Praise 1

Pure Grit *introduces us to individuals who have helped to redefine what is possible. Their stories are educational, inspirational, and aspirational. This book reminds us that what makes us different is a strength — not a liability. I highly recommend it.*

—**DR. RAY BROWNING**, CO-FOUNDER AND CEO OF BIOMOTUM, INC.

Pure Grit *is an authentic and raw look into the life of disability. Collison and Buckley shine a light on the array of misconceptions that people with physical disabilities are forced to endure, while also showcasing a world of unlimited possibility by normalizing disability in a way that is rarely done. The book is a must-read.*

—**JULIE DUSSLIERE**, CHIEF OF PARALYMPIC SPORT, U.S. OLYMPIC & PARALYMPIC COMMITTEE

Pure Grit *is about being determined, but also about being believed in, taking opportunities, having and using support networks, and most importantly, driving social change. Being visible and successful opens a world of possibilities for those who are, and for those who are not, disabled.*

—**DR. CHRISTINE IMMS**, APEX AUSTRALIA CHAIR OF NEURODEVELOPMENT AND DISABILITY, UNIVERSITY OF MELBOURNE, CO-EDITOR OF *PARTICIPATION: OPTIMISING OUTCOMES IN CHILDHOOD-ONSET NEURODISABILITY*

Pure Grit *will encourage our son to own his disability and be all that he is meant to be. A book that also encourages us, as parents, to be bold and brave in how we raise our children. I loved it and can see an immediate difference in how I see and respond to life's challenges.*

—**NICOLA BRASSEY**, TEACHER AND MOTHER TO A CHILD WHO HAS CEREBRAL PALSY, UK

The stories in Pure Grit *are a testament to human achievement no matter your ability. Sports have always been a reflection of our world, and it speaks volumes that so many of these incredible stories are from Paralympians and athletes around the world. An extraordinary read.*

—**CASEY WASSERMAN**, CHAIRPERSON, LOS ANGELES 2028 OLYMPIC AND PARALYMPIC GAMES

Wonderful accounts of individual journeys, sharing unique challenges of physical disability, fuelled by remarkable determination. The horizon of unlimited possibilities for achievement is communicated modestly. One can only be motivated by the unlocking of potential that is highlighted. A compelling read with universal appeal.

—**DR. JANE LEONARD**, MEDICAL DIRECTOR, CRC, DUBLIN

Pure Grit *highlights the lived experience of remarkable individuals, who collectively demonstrate that growing up with a disability brings strength, perspective, and resilience. Importantly, it tells these stories through the lens of the empowerment model rather than the deficit model, demonstrating that disability is a natural, and beautiful, element of diversity and the human experience.*

—**DR. CHERI BLAUWET**, ASSISTANT PROFESSOR OF PM&R, HARVARD MEDICAL SCHOOL; BOARD OF DIRECTORS, U.S. OLYMPIC & PARALYMPIC COMMITTEE AND BOSTON ATHLETIC ASSOCIATION; RETIRED PARALYMPIC WHEELCHAIR RACER.

This remarkable book changes my understanding of the world around me. The personal stories are told with an honesty that gets to the nub of our shared humanity.

—**TOMMIE GORMAN**, IRISH JOURNALIST WHO LIVES WITH CANCER

The authors have a unique ability to meet the storytellers where they are at. Every story is told with an authenticity that gives the reader an opportunity to change the many assumptions they might hold about disability without pushing or instructing them to do so. Each of the nineteen stories is superb in its own right, and as a collection this book is a joy to read.

—**RACHEL BYRNE**, EXECUTIVE DIRECTOR, CEREBRAL PALSY FOUNDATION, NEW YORK

Pure Grit *is a compelling book that takes the reader into the hearts and minds of some extraordinary individuals. The biographies are deeply immersive, often very personal and engaging, yet move the reader to reflect on how lives — who we are and where we are — are so profoundly contingent on our relationship with each other and the culture we inhabit.*

—**DR. EMMA PULLEN**, LECTURER IN SPORTS MANAGEMENT, LOUGHBOROUGH UNIVERSITY, UK

Inspiring! And beautifully told. Every chapter filled with a heart-warming, life-affirming story.

—**JOHN D. MILLER**, FORMER CHIEF MARKETING OFFICER OF NBC SPORTS GROUP

Many clinicians have recognized the value of learning from the experience of disabled youth and adults. Pure Grit *provides that information ... Interviewees recognize that parental, family and community attitudes and the physical environment generate barriers or opportunities to fulfilment in careers and personal life. I highly recommend* Pure Grit *to audiences who are rooting for diversity in all its richness as well as those focused on health and disability studies.*

—**DR. KATHERINE D. SEELMAN**, PROFESSOR EMERITA, UNIVERSITY OF PITTS-BURGH; FORMER DIRECTOR FOR U.S. NATIONAL INSTITUTE ON DISABILITY, INDEPENDENT LIVING, AND REHABILITATION RESEARCH; AND MEMBER OF THE INTERNATIONAL PANEL FOR THE WHO *WORLD REPORT ON DISABILITY*. SHE HAS A HEARING IMPAIRMENT.

Pure Grit *is a necessary read for anyone looking to further disability representation in various storytelling mediums. Not only does it provide helpful insight on how to do so, but more importantly it centers disability within a conversation about the universal truths of how to live a purposeful and fulfilling life. Ultimately, if there is one takeaway from this book, it is: follow your passion.*

—**ASALLE TANHA**, DIRECTOR OF DEVELOPMENT, ORIGINAL SERIES AND MOVIES AT CARTOON NETWORK STUDIOS, LOS ANGELES

This book thoughtfully captures the breadth and diversity of disability in a way that reminds us that disability is an important part of the human experience. Loved the book.

—**BRYAN STROMER**, MARKETING PROFESSIONAL WHO LIVES IN THE U.S., AND WHO HAS CEREBRAL PALSY

This remarkable book prompts us to have courage in the pursuit of our own dreams, and also, to have courage to support others to achieve their life aspirations too — even when challenges are significant. Written in an engaging and accessible format, this book will resonate with and inspire readers, from all walks of life, around the world.

—**DR. ELAINE KINSELLA**, LECTURER IN PSYCHOLOGY, AND RESEARCHER IN HERO-ISM, LEADERSHIP, BRAIN INJURY, UNIVERSITY OF LIMERICK, IRELAND

PURE
GRIT

PURE GRIT

Stories of remarkable people living with physical disability

LILY COLLISON & KARA BUCKLEY

Copyright © 2021 Lily Collison, Kara Buckley, and Gillette Children's Healthcare Press

Gillette Children's Healthcare Press
200 University Avenue East
St. Paul, MN 55101
GilletteChildrensHealthcarePress.org

ISBN 978-1-952181-03-0 (paperback)
ISBN 978-1-952181-04-7 (ebook)
ISBN 978-1-952181-05-4 (audiobook)

Library of Congress Control Number 2021935644

For information about special discounts for bulk purchases, please contact HealthcarePress@gillettechildrens.com

EDITOR Ruth Wilson
COVER AND INTERIOR DESIGNER Jazmin Welch
ILLUSTRATOR Olwyn Roche
AUTHOR PHOTOS Tracy Cepelak
PROJECT MANAGER Carra Simpson
EBOOK PRODUCTION Bright Wing Media
AUDIOBOOK PRODUCTION Central Oregon Recording LLC

*All proceeds from sales of this book will be
donated to physical disability research.*

CONTENTS

PREFACE

IT'S INTERESTING HOW THINGS sometimes happen in our lives by chance.

I've known Kara, coauthor of this book, for a number of years. Kara suggested to me that I might like to read *Struggling with Serendipity*, a book written by Cindy Kolbe about life following a car accident that left her fourteen-year-old daughter Beth paralyzed. Beth later graduated from Harvard University and represented the U.S. at the Beijing 2008 Paralympic Games. Beth applied to Harvard only after catching sight of a billboard on the side of a highway — the billboard showed a Harvard student in a wheelchair wearing a graduation gown.

For Beth, that billboard shined a light on what is possible.

I have personal experience of people growing up with physical disability — my youngest son, Tommy, has spastic diplegia, a common type of cerebral palsy (CP). This led me to writing the book, *Spastic Diplegia—Bilateral Cerebral Palsy*. In writing it, I read many academic papers, but one, written by a Dutch research group, made a lasting impression on me.[1] It showed that compared with the general population, people with spastic diplegia (also known as bilateral cerebral palsy) have lower rates of employment, relationships, and having children. Research from other countries also bears out this finding. It really bothered me that people with just a mild/moderate physical disability with no cognitive impairment (as spastic diplegia generally is) have lower rates of participation in society.

An Australian initiative, CP-Achieve,[2] aims to address the health and social inequities of adolescents and young adults with cerebral palsy. Learning about the great work they were doing, I felt there was a need for role models — people living with physical disability who have achieved in different areas of life. Just one example is Daniel Dias, a Brazilian Paralympic swimmer who has won multiple medals. In an interview, he credited fellow Paralympian Clodoaldo Silva for getting him into the sport: "I only began because I saw Clodoaldo swimming on television. I didn't know people like me could swim, could do any sport at all."[3]

Another is Justin Gallegos, who is the first professional athlete with cerebral palsy to be signed by Nike. He shows what is possible when living with a disability.

Within a month of Kara recommending that I read Cindy Kolbe's book, I suggested to her that we cowrite this book. Beth, Daniel, and Justin are just three people featured in it; sixteen others tell their stories, too. The aim of the book is to shine a light on remarkable people living with physical disability.

–**Lily Collison**

. . .

When I asked the chief of U.S. Paralympic Sport, Julie Dussliere, to recommend a biography of a Paralympian, she suggested I read *Struggling with Serendipity*. The book had a major impact on me, as both a mom and a sports executive. I recommended the book to Lily, and fed off her enthusiasm when we later spoke. She stressed the need to tell more stories about people who grew up with disabilities to serve as "that billboard" for others. During our conversation, she raised the idea of us cowriting this book.

I was immediately interested. The idea of writing such a book aligned with one common thread that has been constant in my career — working at the intersection of human perseverance and excellence in sport, to be a champion for athletes regardless of their individual challenge, be it due to age, gender, nationality, or physical disability. Previously, when I was working at Visa, I pioneered the Rio 2016 acceptance campaign supporting all ten athletes on the Refugee Olympic Team. Today, one in three athletes I work with has a physical disability, and one of my goals is to democratize athlete access to opportunities, especially between Paralympians and Olympians.

While we have made a lot of progress within the Paralympic Movement, there is still room for improvement. For example, in the United States, several elite feeder programs exist for Olympic sport, but there is often no clear path for many children and teenagers with physical disabilities to train for the Paralympics. Through the stories in this book, I saw the potential to focus more attention on developing a path for young people with physical disabilities to pursue sport.

In the recent Netflix documentary *Rising Phoenix*, Paralympian Ellie Cole talks about having her leg amputated as a young child — she explains that she didn't have any role models to look up to until she learned about the Paralympic Games. This comment on lack of role models mirrors conversations I've had with other Paralympians.

Lily and I both share the philosophy of living with a growth mindset and a spirit of optimism: that you may not be able to control what happens to you in life, but you can control how you react.

I soon realized how a book like this could be useful.

–Kara Buckley

· · ·

Together, we wrote the stories in this book by doing background research and then both of us interviewing each participant over Zoom. We Zoomed around the world from Campinas in Brazil to Sydney in Australia to Reykjavík in Iceland, having a lot of fun connecting across time zones.

In telling each story, we have respected each individual's preferred disability language — some prefer "disabled person," rather than "person with disability," and "nondisabled person" rather than "able-bodied person."

No conclusions are drawn — we leave it to you, the reader, to draw your own.

We've also included two appendices with further information and context: Appendix 1 provides resources to learn more about physical disabilities. Appendix 2 contains information on Para sport.

We hope that the stories in this book might nudge all of us — disabled and nondisabled — to reflect on how we are living our lives. The stories shine a light on boundless possibility whatever our individual challenge.

–Lily Collison and Kara Buckley

INTRODUCTION

THIS BOOK TELLS STORIES of remarkable people living with physical disability — adults who have grown up with a physical disability from birth or acquired one during childhood or adolescence, and who have achieved much in their individual fields.

An estimated two to three percent of children and adolescents grow up with a physical disability,[1] which is a different experience from acquiring one in adulthood, when one is already established as a person. For the child and adolescent with a physical disability, the challenge of their disability is added to all the "regular" challenges of growing up. It is worth noting, though, that as people progress through adulthood, they may acquire physical disability through, for example, accident or illness. Disability is a reality for fifteen percent of people *across the lifespan*. A billion people worldwide have a disability.[2]

The people in these stories are remarkable in different ways — they are successful across fields such as business, sport, medicine, dance, tech, and politics. The sports stories are varied, but a number of them feature swimmers (reflecting the popularity of swimming as a sport of choice for people with a physical disability).

These are stories of people with different types of physical disabilities. Since cerebral palsy (CP) is the most common cause of physical disability in childhood,[3] several stories feature people with this condition — and where known we have specified the type (spastic diplegia or hemiplegia). These stories also address physical disability alone, acknowledging that some physical disabilities also have associated cognitive challenges.

Although the stories are diverse, some common themes emerge. Many tell of parents being given poor predictions of their child's life soon after birth. "Won't." "Can't." "Never." These words were often heard.

But these people have lived out a different story. These remarkable individuals are not *overcoming* disability — they are accommodating disability in their lives while pursuing their dreams. Many tell of influential people they had early in their lives, and all offer rich insights on disability. For instance, just because a person has a disability doesn't mean they are exceptional, special, or inspirational — they are ordinary. It is what they *do* in life that makes them remarkable.

Athletes talk of wanting to be recognized for their sporting achievements, not to be given inspirational awards merely for participating. Others emphasize that the environment (physical and attitudinal) is often more limiting than the disability itself; that sometimes, nondisabled people are uncomfortable around disability simply because they don't know any disabled people. Giving disability visibility is important.

Perseverance is the one characteristic that all the people in these stories share — they all display *pure grit*, which is what inspired the title of the book. In her story, Ila Eckhoff says, "Grit is one of those things that we don't quite know how to measure. Grit has been proven to have much more of an impact on goals, objectives, and achievement — even more than intellect . . . a person with above-average grit is going to go a lot further than somebody who's super smart with zero grit who, once they get stopped, doesn't know how to get back up." Everyone profiled in this book knows, or has learned, how to get up again.

And while many of those featured in these stories don't see themselves as role models, they are. Role models, as most people understand, have a useful place in society, and a growing body of research supports their importance.[4]

Success in life is to some extent additive — later success builds on earlier successes and failures. The remarkable people featured here vary in age from their twenties to seventies and are at different stages of success. For example, in Paralympic sport, one athlete has just made the qualifying time; others are world-leading multi-medalists.

Taken together, the stories shine a light on unlimited possibilities. Success is what *you* want it to be. Success is achievement at any age. Success can be in the quiet of your own home as equally as on a world stage. Success takes effort, success takes resilience, and indeed, sometimes success takes failure. Success can bring satisfaction, and success "breeds success."

Reading this book will make you laugh and sometimes cry. The book goes a long way toward dispelling the lingering myth that disability is something to be pitied, that it leads to a "less than" life. When reading these stories, pity is not likely the emotion you will feel — more likely it will be awe and, indeed, sometimes envy of these amazingly fulfilled and vibrant lives.

Marian Wright Edelman, the American activist for children's rights, coined the phrase: "You can't be what you can't see." We hope this book will help people *see* in order *to be*.

LEX GILLETTE

No need for sight when you have a vision

Lex is a U.S. Paralympic long jumper.
He has been blind since childhood.

LEX GILLETTE STEPS OFF THE SCHOOL BUS, feeling the firm pavement under his feet as the warm spring air hits his face. A backpack in tow, he steps up onto the curb of the familiar sidewalk, walking straight. He reaches the grass line, feeling the soft padding beneath his shoes, his cue to turn right. Because Lex cannot see, his daily journey home from school is guided by his other senses.

Lex arrives at the stairs, counting the steps — one, two, three — before taking five steps forward. He then has a choice: he can turn right toward his front door or, even better, he can turn left, to the ledge.

That beloved ledge represents freedom to this young boy from Raleigh, North Carolina. Lex drops his backpack, picks up his pace, and runs. His arms spread wide as he pushes off the edge, jumps, and starts to fly. Gravity draws him three feet down, landing on the soft grass below.

Lex was not born blind. He still remembers the sight of flowers blooming and birds flying in his neighborhood. It wasn't until he was three years old that he first lost vision in his left eye due to a detached retina. He still had vision in his right eye though — until things started to go murky at age eight.

Once again, a detached retina was the culprit. When Lex got into the bathtub one night, he saw lines blurring his vision, and the next day at school, teachers noticed that he was bumping into things in the classroom. Lex had to wear an eye patch for several weeks and began a series of new operations.

"After the tenth operation (I endured thirteen starting at three years old), ophthalmologist Dr. Brooks McKewen talked to my mother. He said to her, 'Ms. Gillette, we have tried everything. Your son will eventually go blind. I am sorry, but there is nothing else we can do.' Questions rattled around in my head. 'So, now what?' I wondered," Lex later wrote in his memoir.[1]

His mother, Verdina, had already instilled her own approach to navigating disability into Lex's hard drive. She is also visually impaired, having a form of glaucoma that grants her some usable sight. She was Lex's role model early on.

"She was a really good example," says Lex. "I think the biggest thing is that she let me go, at the end of the day. She let me go outside and discover and continue to explore after I lost my sight. Although I couldn't see anything, it was about learning the neighborhood from my other senses."

With his mother's blend of expectations and aspirations, Lex quickly learned how to navigate independently. Verdina expected Lex to have the same responsibilities as any other kid: washing the dishes, doing his chores, and finishing his homework. She aspired for him to gain autonomy, encouraging him to learn how to navigate life among his sighted peers.

"It was literally my mom who kept me growing, allowing me to go out there and figure out the world from all aspects, minus the visual," says Lex. "She told me 'This is your life. I want you to be able to go into the world and do amazing things. I want you to achieve everything you see within your mind, and it doesn't matter what anyone says or the obstacles that lie in your path. You have what it takes internally to over-come all of those things.'"

Verdina never cocooned or overprotected Lex. She let him try new things. Other people would come over and see Lex outside, doing cartwheels and jumping, and say, "Oh my gosh, he's going to kill himself!" But his mom would defend the freedom she allowed, countering that she had to let him.

Her penchant for encouraging Lex's independence came from a core truth: that without sight, he made up only a small percentage of people in the world, and she never wanted him to be completely separated from the larger population. She knew that when he went out into the world, especially as an adult, the majority of people would be able to see. So, she wanted to keep him embedded in mainstream society — par-ticipating, interacting, and working alongside sighted peers.

Verdina made a deliberate decision early on to keep Lex in public school, integrated with sighted children. It took Lex a year to learn braille in elementary school. He was given text-books in braille and began using a braille writer, much like an old-fashioned typewriter. Homework took longer for him to do than it did for his peers. Fortunately, Lex didn't experience much bullying as a child. Kids joked, but he quickly learned to joke as well. By dishing it back, he showed kids he wouldn't put up with it, and they stopped picking on him. He kept things as light and friendly as possible.

Every summer, Lex attended programs at a local school for the blind, which offered courses on independent living and mobility. There he learned how to care for himself at a young age — how to iron his clothes, do laundry, clean the house — a host of practical skills that he still uses today. In elementary school, Lex also started working with a mobility specialist, John Higgins, who taught him how to use a cane to "see" his surroundings in place of his eyes. Higgins created three-dimensional maps so Lex could read directions: gluing down sticks to paper so he could feel the roads with his hands, and using braille to name each street. The map pointed to Lex's favorite restaurant, T.J. Cinnamons, with a reward of cinnamon buns for navigating the neighborhood autonomously.

As he did in his lessons with Mr. Higgins, Lex learned from his mother an important philosophy: there is a difference between sight and vision. While his sight was limited, Verdina maintained a strong vision for the wonderful, independent life her son could — and would go on to — have, though never imagining the level of success he would find in sport and public speaking.

• • •

As he was when jumping off the ledge, Lex is freest while in motion. On summer breaks from school, he enjoyed that freedom riding bikes with his cousins during visits to the countryside where they lived.

They never focused on the fact that he couldn't see anything. Instead, they adapted and made accommodations to include Lex. At that age, no one deliberately thought about "inclusion," but of course, as humans, kids figure it out.

As Lex would pedal down the road with his cousins, he could hear the gravel crunch beneath his tires. He followed the similar crunching sound from the bike ahead — his cousin leading the way down the rural lane in the July sun. The smell of pine trees enveloped Lex, with a humid heat radiating from the ground. Hearing his cousin take a right, Lex would mimic the movement, and the path would audibly change. A soft, smooth sound indicated they were now on the dirt path heading back to the house.

"Every aspect of life has a certain sound to it," says Lex. "I knew that if I was in line with where they were, then that would keep me in a really safe space."

Lex got creative when navigating other sports too. It was basketball that changed his life.

In North Carolina, basketball is a religion. Lex was a huge Michael Jordan and Tar Heels fan, so it was a no-brainer — of course he'd play the game, too, shooting hoops in his childhood bedroom, with a Nerf net hung on the back of his door. Lex oriented his room around that net, knowing the position of his bed and dresser relative to the door, so he could envisage where it was located. He spent hours shooting basket after basket, and it got to the point where he literally felt like he could see what was going on.

"I knew that if I could shoot this basket — something I couldn't see — I could shoot for anything else in life," says Lex. "I transferred that same type of energy to my outlook on life. It really helped me to put the rubber to the road. I think that's a very important lesson nowadays, that to achieve things it does take hours and hours of practice."

That net became a symbol for Lex. It signified a goal he had set for himself and taught him a lesson in confidence: that with determination and practice he could achieve great things, despite being blind.

In high school, he joined the track-and-field team and quickly progressed to international competitions, going to his first Paralympics in Athens in 2004. Lex competed in the long jump and won his first silver medal there at age nineteen.

· · ·

In the long jump, Lex's guide, Wesley Williams, stands at the end of the runway, clapping and shouting to direct Lex.

When Wesley begins to clap, Lex heads in his direction at full speed, and starts counting his strides. After Lex plants his foot on the sixteenth step, he hears Wesley shouting, "Fly, fly, fly," as Lex leaps in the air. Lex's feet leave the pavement and come down together as he lands in the sandpit. In competition, medals aren't just awarded to the athletes competing — guides also receive a medal.

In Paralympic sport, Lex is classified as T11 — T for track events, and 11 to indicate vision impairment and its level. All T11 athletes are required to wear eyeshades to ensure a fair competition, since some have reduced vision while others have no vision at all. The irony, of course, is that in Lex's case, he has shaped his entire career on the fact that his blindness is *not* an impairment. Through sport, and lessons from his mother, Lex has found that he is no longer imprisoned by what is and has instead gained the ability to see what could be.

...

Lex attended East Carolina University, a massive campus with 20,000 students. There he learned how to use the help offered from Disability Services and other resources to ensure his academic success. In those life transitions, Lex learned how to advocate for himself. He no longer had his mom to speak up on his behalf.

"It was a totally different situation. I had to be vulnerable and verbalize the types of assistance I needed," says Lex. "I was still dealing with different insecurities about my blindness, wondering if I was looking toward someone when I was speaking to them, or if people were looking at me weirdly."

He got over those feelings of awkwardness by learning how to push through. Lex came to understand that by having the courage to open himself up and ask for what he needed, he could get over his nervousness. Whenever he took a step forward, the feelings started to dissipate. He realized he didn't get hurt, nothing crazy happened — and he was able to achieve what he needed. It encouraged him to keep going.

When he was younger, Lex had observed his mother push through similar tough situations. As a single mom, Verdina was the model of the characteristics that she wanted to pass on to Lex: warm, hardworking, and meticulous. Money wasn't plentiful, but Lex never lacked in family love and support. Although Verdina and Lex's father were no longer together, his mom encouraged Lex to have a relationship with his dad. The two of them spent every summer together, and when Lex's dad passed away in 2010, Lex found peace in their relationship and the knowledge that his father was immensely proud of him.

Lex's relationship with both of his parents taught him to be attuned to habits that develop strength and resilience. Once he was on his own, he used that same power of observation to his benefit: how to pick and choose habits from other people. Lex saw how people balanced certain aspects of their lives, and he adopted the habits that worked for him.

One of the habits he rejected from the get-go was expecting instant gratification. Growing up, Lex saw many wonderful advancements for visually impaired people, like Aira, an app that he now uses to connect with a sighted person via his smartphone camera anytime he needs extra assistance.[2] But with such advancements also comes a shift in how we all operate and think. We have all become programmed to expect immediate results.

"In a way, success is challenging because people look at opportunities and the trajectory of life in the same way," Lex says. "People need to understand that success takes time.

And it's going to take some falling down to figure out how to get back up."

Lex has learned that nothing can be achieved alone. In long jump, every competition requires teamwork. Lex knows that the first step in winning is realizing that you need other people in order to transform your vision into reality.

. . .

On a warm, summer day in London, Lex kicks his leg high into the air, touching his toe to his fingertips. Finishing his warmup, he walks into the holding zone and takes a seat. He hears the familiar sounds of his competitors: lilts of Portuguese among the Brazilian team, stochastic tones from the Chinese delegation. Officials check Lex's bag, ensuring his spikes meet competition standards.

Suddenly it's go time. Lex rises and is escorted into the tunnel. As he walks forward, he feels the concrete beneath his shoes begin to incline. The people speaking in foreign languages around him hush as the group progresses toward the mouth of the stadium, feeling a contagious sense of mounting anticipation. Lex quietly reflects on his preparation — Every. Single. Day. — for the previous four years, all leading to this point.

In the same instant that Lex feels the sun hit his face, he feels the rubberized mondo track under his feet. In a dramatic flash, tens of thousands of people surround him — screaming for him, screaming against him.

The London 2012 Paralympic Games feel like home.

"I started clapping my hands. The next thing you know, 85,000 people started clapping their hands in the exact same rhythm. That was the essence of unity," says Lex. "At that moment, we all had the same heartbeat. I could relive that moment over and over again."

Lex's career in sport is full of impressive accomplishments — most notably, as the best totally blind long and triple jumper in the history of the U.S. Paralympic Movement. In addition, he's the current world record holder in long jump, a four-time Paralympic medalist, four-time long jump world champion, and eighteen-time national champion.

It doesn't stop there. Lex is also musically gifted: playing the piano, singing and even recording his own songs. He published his first book in 2020, *Fly*, a memoir. Lex Gillette Day is celebrated on September 25 in both Hagerstown and Washington County in Maryland. And he is in high demand as a motivational speaker, talking to audiences about the difference between sight and vision.

Lex uses the lessons he has learned in sport to create analogies that apply to business and leadership. He takes his experience of leaping blindly into the sand and repurposes that into helping other people leap into new opportunities in their own lives.

His legacy is already in motion. Lex is a mentor for children through Classroom Champions, an organization that pairs elite athletes with classrooms to teach kids important lessons. He remembers how important it was to have his own role models at a young age, and he provides those same lessons he learned — about goal setting, perseverance, and healthy living.

"A lot of us want change, but it has to happen within ourselves. There's a lot that we personally have to do as we push forward in life," Lex says. "And a lot of the change we want to see in the world depends on how we raise the future generation.

"And so, working with Classroom Champions and being able to equip these kids with great skills is about wanting to build this world that I feel will produce a lot of success."

• • •

Lex finds motivation in knowing our time on Earth is finite. His ultimate goal is to exhaust every aspect of his entire being. He wants to soak up every opportunity in life so at the end, he can say that he didn't leave anything in the tank.

He's also driven to leave something on this Earth that wasn't here before. A big part of that legacy is his definition of vision — and our ability to see things before they exist. He wants to open people's eyes and minds to the potential that lies within. And he wants to pay it forward, using everything he's been blessed with to share opportunities with others.

"I want to break down barriers for the next person," says Lex. "Especially when we look at the Paralympic Movement. Since I started in 2004, I've seen how it has evolved, driven by all these pioneers. I want to help too. The next athletes that come along shouldn't have to fight the same battles. I want to clear up some of those bottlenecks now, to make their lives easier and help keep the Movement flourishing."

Lex says one of the challenges in the U.S. is a lack of understanding about Paralympic sport. A big part of that is getting mainstream media and corporations to put the Paralympics at the forefront, showing the amazing athletic talents across a variety of sports — from swimmers to wheelchair rugby to sitting volleyball. He sees the Los Angeles 2028 Paralympic Games as an opportunity to change those perceptions and make things explode in a positive way.

"All of these sports have these amazing athletes. When you start to dig deeper, you learn about who they are as humans, and the things they do off the field of play," says Lex.

"These are the things people need to see. Yes, we have a disability, but that doesn't inhibit us from any other aspect of life. We're still successful. We hold down jobs, and support families. We have kids.

"I want the public to see how we're participating in life."

Lex knows that to evolve public perception, he must start with his vision for change — an image, a belief, a dream for how the world sees Paralympians. And with that vision, he can change the world.

JAN BRUNSTROM-HERNANDEZ

Meant to live

Based in Texas, "Dr. Jan" is a pediatric neurologist specializing in cerebral palsy care. She has spastic diplegia.

AN ANNUAL CONFERENCE at Pacific Lutheran University (PLU) in Tacoma, Washington, brings alumni back to talk with current students. The 2015 keynote speaker, Dr. Jan Brunstrom-Hernandez, a 1983 graduate, walks to the podium to deliver her presentation, titled Meant to Live.

She tells the audience that she has cerebral palsy because she was born three months early, weighing a little over three pounds. Her parents had previously lost multiple pregnancies through both miscarriages and premature births.

Doctors had told her mother that she would not get pregnant again. When she did, the doctors said the pregnancy would not go to term. When Jan was born, doctors said she had no chance of survival. After she did survive, they said that she would never walk or talk.

Dr. Jan Brunstrom-Hernandez, or "Dr. Jan," as she's affectionately known by her patient families, is a pediatric neurologist and an internationally recognized expert in cerebral palsy. Dr. Jan understands cerebral palsy because she has been both a researcher and clinician in this field. She also understands it because she has lived with cerebral palsy and has defied each one of those early predictions.

Dr. Jan has the spastic diplegic form of cerebral palsy; it mostly affects her lower limbs, but she has some upper limb involvement.

Dr. Jan was born in Seattle. She has a sister who is just six weeks older who was adopted at birth. Her parents had pursued adoption before her mother became pregnant with Jan. At that time, one couldn't adopt if pregnant, but a court case allowed the already-initiated adoption process to continue, since the expectations for the pregnancy to reach viability were so low.

Her dad, who always traveled a lot for work, didn't leave the city once for the entire time Jan was in the hospital after her birth. "He came to see me every day and took movies with a reel-to-reel camera through a glass partition." She explains, "When, as an adult, I asked him why he went to all the trouble to take movies of me when he was told I had zero chance of survival, he said he wanted to document that he had a baby girl."

Her mother, on the other hand, couldn't bear to come to the hospital because she didn't want to get attached to another baby the doctors predicted would die. She had had too many losses, including a baby boy who was born prematurely and died the day he was due to be brought home from the hospital. Dr. Jan believes that fear of loss had a lifelong effect on her mother, and on their mother–daughter relationship.

The pregnancy losses over a decade took a toll on both her parents. Of her dad, she says, "The thing that was stuck in his heart, even as I grew to be an adult, was hearing doctors say I had zero chance of survival. That caused such an incredible heartache and sadness in him, which I'm not sure he has ever been able to let go of.

"When I eventually came home from the hospital around two months old, I was not developing normally and was stiff as a board. Nobody would tell my parents what was wrong. Everything was blamed on my being premature."

Her parents were overwhelmed. "Thankfully, my grandmother stepped in saying, 'I'm going to stand her up; I'm going to do stuff with her.'"

When Jan was still a baby, her dad's job took the family initially to England and then to Australia. England was where Jan was diagnosed, when she was eighteen months old, when a doctor, who was treating her sister looked at Jan's mom and said, "Do you know that the child sitting on your lap has cerebral palsy?"

Dr. Jan says, "My mom's reaction was, 'thankfully, somebody has finally told me.'"

Now armed with a diagnosis, her mom was determined to find ways to help. "She encouraged me to do a lot of standing. She insisted that when I fell down, I would always pick myself up. I had piano lessons to help my weak left hand. She was very against surgery, because she was terrified of anesthesia and also because she feared a bad outcome," Dr. Jan says. "My mother was strong and very determined, but I don't ever remember her hugging me as a child."

Jan attended the Spastic Centre in Perth (one of the locations of Spastic Centre Australia, an organization she would in later life collaborate with as the renamed Cerebral Palsy Alliance). It was there she received both therapy and schooling. Though Dr. Jan doesn't remember this, her mom credits a teacher there who clearly looked at the whole child — a teacher who believed in Jan and who taught her to read at age four.

"My mother was also a teacher, but because of what everybody had told her about cerebral palsy, she thought I was cognitively impaired. It would be many years later, when I was graduating from high school at age sixteen, first in my class, that my mother, crying, told me she was very sorry that she didn't fully believe I was okay. Right up to the moment when she found out I was first in my class, she still had her doubts."

Her mom says she should have known better when Jan came home reading at the age of four. But as Dr. Jan points out, "Just because teaching is your profession doesn't mean that you take your blinders off and see your own child objectively."

When Jan was seven, the family moved back to the U.S. Her parents had difficulty finding a school that could provide appropriate education and therapy like they had found in Australia. They tried public school, but ended up sending her to private school.

Her parents went on to adopt two more children. When Jan was sixteen, her parents divorced. Her dad later remarried, and she has a brother from that relationship.

• • •

Jan wanted to be a doctor from the time she was six years old. She started down that path at just sixteen, enrolling in PLU to study for a bachelor of science in biology. She succeeded, but it wasn't all plain sailing. An early academic advisor suggested she "go home and grow up; you're way too young to be in college."

She ignored this advice.

During her senior year in college she applied to medical schools. It was 1983, and discrimination raised its head at one interview. Given her physical disability, she was questioned about her suitability to be a doctor. Would she risk a baby's life? What if she dropped a baby while walking? Her calm and well-reasoned reply to the questions about her disability ensured she passed that particular interview.

Dr. Jan graduated from Virginia Commonwealth University in 1987 and then did her pediatric neurology training at St. Louis Children's Hospital and Barnes–Jewish Hospital, neighboring hospitals in St. Louis. She went on to complete a postdoctoral research fellowship in developmental neurobiology at Washington University School of Medicine, in St. Louis, before joining the faculty there in 1995.

During this time, she married and had a son. She spoke of her joy in motherhood in her 2015 presentation at PLU: "I got to have a baby, even though all the doctors said that I would never have a baby. Why? Not because there was anything wrong with my insides. It was because I had cerebral palsy. When you have cerebral palsy, there's this big box and everything that goes wrong with you gets dumped in this box and people make assumptions. I did have a baby and I gave birth to him in the regular way, and I'm happy to say he is perfectly healthy."[1]

Dr. Jan's son, Ian, now in his mid-twenties, is a professional musician. Dr. Jan says, "My son is a very good musician. I mean, I'm biased but he's very talented." She herself is musical, and if she hadn't become a doctor, she says her career choice might have been in the music business. She adds with a smile, "I live vicariously through my son."

• • •

In 1998, Dr. Jan founded and became the director of the Pediatric Neurology Cerebral Palsy Center at Washington University School of Medicine and St. Louis Children's Hospital, a position she held for over sixteen years.

She had been initially reluctant to start the clinic, despite strong and continuous encouragement from her colleagues. She confesses she struggled to accept her own disability. She has said that "The biggest reason I didn't want to start a clinic was because I was too uncomfortable around kids who were like me. I'd gotten so good at 'forgetting' my disability except when I fell down and things like that. I also tried to protect other people from my disability . . . I would try to make it okay for them not to feel uncomfortable."[1]

She freely admits now that the clinic — and especially the children — changed her life. Learning from her patients and families, she grew to accept herself and make peace with her disability. She says, "When I started the clinic, I was working very hard at trying to be good enough. Meanwhile, I had these patients and their families saying to me, 'Thank you, Dr. Jan. We love you Dr. Jan.' They would give me hugs and I wasn't feeling very huggable at that point. They would say things like, 'You're so great. You've helped us so much.'

"All I could think was — if you really knew me you wouldn't say that because I'm the crippled kid that nobody ever wanted to go out with, that nobody ever wanted . . .

"I was mad at the world because I felt I had to prove myself all the time and at a different level than typically developing people. I had not only to prove myself academically to be able to be a doctor, but I also had to prove to myself that I could be even better because they're all looking at my disability. I was this bitter, angry person, but most people couldn't tell this because I was always putting on a smile.

"But they broke down the wall. They cracked through the veneer. The kids and their families taught me that I can be okay the way that I am — even if I never walk better — even if I never walk perfectly. They taught me unconditional love and acceptance of myself exactly the way that I am. I didn't have to be one iota better to be loved by them. It was because of these children and their families that I started to heal and become a real person capable of loving someone else."

Dr. Jan is quick to point how much, even to this day, she learns from her patients and their families. She is also very quick to acknowledge the wonderful staff who worked at the St. Louis clinic, adding that treating kids with cerebral palsy is a team effort.

As well as the clinic staff, Dr. Jan also acknowledges the great support she received from other colleagues in St. Louis and around the world.

• • •

One of the remarkable aspects of the St. Louis clinic is its sports program for children and adolescents with cerebral palsy. The program offers a wide range of sports — martial arts, swimming, dance, tennis, baseball, volleyball, soccer, and basketball. Camp Independence is the intensive summer sports program, but there are activities year-round. The program is run by a physical therapist, and family members (of both patients and staff) are enthusiastic volunteers.

Dr. Jan says that getting kids with cerebral palsy into sport is very important. "Sport is really great therapy. Learning to play sport themselves also got the kids playing with their family and friends. Sport really opened the eyes of these kids and changed their lives."

Getting the chance to participate herself in sports was a bonus for Dr. Jan, as she had never played sports growing up. In her forties, she learned to play basketball, water-ski, and dance, and she discovered that certain dance rhythms reduced her dystonia. She got her first bike, a recumbent model, and experienced for the first time the pleasure of riding with her son, and the joy kids get from going fast on a bike.

She emphasizes that "older people with cerebral palsy can also learn new motor skills."

For the work she did in St. Louis, Dr. Jan was named Outstanding Missourian of the Year in 2007. And two months before she left Missouri for her next career challenge, the mayor of St. Louis proclaimed October 1, 2014, as Dr. Jan Brunstrom-Hernandez Day.

...

Dr. Jan now resides in the Dallas–Fort Worth area in Texas, where she moved with her second husband, Ruben, a Texan, to set up her own cerebral palsy treatment center — 1 CP Place. This was the realization of a dream of hers to set up a freestanding clinic with the mission to help young people with cerebral palsy "live their very best, healthiest lives."

With the help of a very committed team, Dr. Jan coordinates the care of the children and adolescents with cerebral palsy, many whose photographs adorn the clinic hallways. Ruben, who made Dr. Jan's dream his dream, manages the technology and office administration. (Unfortunately, for now, COVID-19 has curtailed the clinic's sports program.)

Dr. Jan won't listen to any negative predictions about any kid with cerebral palsy. She's realistic and knows that they won't all do wonderfully, but she says, "I promise you that every single child, every single person can do much better than the negative expectations that have been leveled at them, so that's what I was put here to do.

"My job is to find all the available information and do a very thorough examination of each kid and figure out what the problems are, what the strengths are and what we can do to help them right now."

Families have different reactions to learning that their child has a disability. "Some have this ability to accept their child exactly like they are right now," Dr. Jan says. "They'll explain, 'We love our child just like they are. You don't have to fix everything, but if there's something you can do to make their quality of life better . . .' There are also parents who want you to pull out all the stops and make their child perfect. In some ways, I could relate to the latter type because for a long time I worked to be perfect myself — it wasn't going to happen.

"Parents want predictions from me all the time, 'Are they going to walk?' My answer is, 'Well, we're sure going to try,' or if it looks really tough, I say, 'We're going to try, but here are the obstacles they're up against,' and I explain, 'Your child will let you know. We just have to wait. We just have to give it a little bit more time and then we will see.' You have to give the parents time to come to grips with it, and you have to give the child a chance to show what they can do, because the motivation of the child counts for a lot."

While her priority at the clinic is to treat children and adolescents, Dr. Jan also treats adults, acknowledging the lack of care for adults with cerebral palsy.

In addition to treating all her patients, she considers it her job "to go nag and poke and push all these other doctors and scientists and smart people to do their very best so that we can have more options and more treatments and that, some day, we will have cures!" To that end, she herself has contributed to the research as coauthor of over twenty publications. She has also written chapters for a number of books.

• • •

Dr. Jan speaks directly to others living with a disability, sharing her wisdom from what she has learned herself from having cerebral palsy and later life challenges. She knows that the biggest limitations with having a physical disability are not physical environmental things like curb cuts or inaccessible buildings: "It's the inaccessibility of most of the world's minds about what people [with disability] can and cannot do."[1] She advises people with disability to "just don't take no for an answer."

She understands that "everything takes longer. It takes me more time to do the daily life stuff, so I have less time. For example, I'm slower walking, getting dressed, and typing."

An added challenge for her has been the diagnosis of rheumatoid arthritis, which came when she was in her forties. She says, "It took two years to diagnose because I kept being told that it was due to my cerebral palsy." It was a hard lesson for this very independent woman to admit: "I finally had to let someone help me. I finally had to say I can't do it all by myself."

Through it all, she's learned a lot of lessons and grown in wisdom:

"Find *your* calling," she says. "Identify and play to your strengths to be the best *you* that you can be; make the biggest contribution you can to this world, to help people for generations to come.

"It's not about being 'perfect physically' because that's almost never possible; it's about being physically fit, healthy, and pain free.

"Live a full life. That includes trying and failing at relationships; going after a dream and risk failing; not having stuff given to you just because you have a disability.

"Never feel shame for something you have no control over. Never feel you can't be beautiful just because you walk funny, like I do. Beauty comes from within. It's okay to want to change, it's okay to want to do things better, once it comes from a place of acceptance, of having made peace with your disability."

She recalls a time from her childhood that she has never forgotten: "I was around seven and the principal at the school videotaped all the kids at school to show at a fundraiser. I could never truly run, but I could kind of move fast and do this waddling kind of movement. The video clip showed me trying to run down the hall grinning from ear to ear, I'm very happy in the clip.

"When the video was shown, the auditorium erupted in laughter at the scene with me in it. I sat in that auditorium feeling only shame. I stopped trying to run that day, but I never stopped wanting to run."

The moral of that story is, "The value of a person is not defined by what they look like or how they move."

Dr. Jan asks, "How do we teach that? How do we teach kids to be strong when they are mocked or bullied? In a world of social media messages going viral, how do we teach them resilience?"

• • •

Dr. Jan has defied the many negative predictions ascribed to her. In helping kids with cerebral palsy and their families, she has found her calling.

She was *meant to live*.

DANIEL DIAS

Smile for life

Daniel is a Brazilian Paralympic swimmer and was born with incompletely formed limbs.

DANIEL DIAS WAS BORN a month before his due date, in Campinas, Brazil, in 1988. When his mother, Rosana, was pregnant, she didn't have a prenatal ultrasound because it was too expensive, so it was a surprise to everyone when Daniel was born with incompletely formed upper and lower limbs. The doctors placed Daniel in an incubator, and as soon as Rosana had recovered from the delivery, she went to see him. She drew close and whispered, "Hi son. Mommy is here." At that very moment, Daniel smiled back at her.

Daniel says, "She tells me that when she saw that smile, she didn't care if there were arms, legs, or if there weren't. She saw that smile, and I honestly believe God was telling her, 'Look, it's going to be all right. We'll live it day by day.' And that was exactly how my parents managed, day by day."

The story of his birth inspired Daniel's personal mantra: *Smile for life.* He believes that through a smile, you can transform someone's life, just like what happened when he smiled at his mom when she visited him in the nursery.

"I smiled at her and she didn't see the disability. She saw a smile from her baby. Sometimes words can't say as much as a smile," says Daniel. "I believe in the power of a smile. In being able to look at someone and not knowing at times what they're going through. But being able to smile at them

— maybe that's exactly what they need that day. And that smile will make a difference in their life.

"The first person I smile at every day is myself, when I wake up and look at myself in the mirror. When we see a smile, it cheers us up. So, smile at yourself! And then go chase your dreams, your goals."

• • •

When Daniel was young, his goals were similar to those of any child's: learn how to tie shoelaces, ride a bike, play the drums. While it took him longer than other children, he accomplished exactly what he set out to do — learning how to adapt with his limbs, with the wonderful support of his parents.

"My parents never put a limit on what I was capable of doing and achieving in my life," says Daniel. "And to this day when I talk to my mom about it, I'll ask her, 'Mom, how did you teach me to do certain things, like the simple act of tying my shoes?' And she'll say, 'Honestly, I would show you something and before I realized it, you were doing it. I would ask you to make your bed and you would go and do it. Most of the time I forgot you didn't have your arms.'

"I would just go and get things done. Everyone falls when they learn how to ride a bike. I fell too. It wasn't because I didn't have any hands. So that's exactly how I would define my early childhood: my parents never setting any limits on what I was capable of."

Daniel's learning how to ride a bike wasn't exactly fast, though. It took time and patience and perseverance. But with his parents' belief that he could do it, he did.

"The most important thing is to persevere and not give up. And my parents were able to discern that, adopting the attitude, 'My kid can do it in his own time. It won't be easy — it will be a great challenge, a great obstacle — but he can do it.'

"I think what they did was unique: to believe in their son. When I tell you that they never put a limit on what I could achieve, that's exactly what I mean."

The same unwavering confidence helped Daniel when he went to preschool. "My first day at school was a very hard one for me," he says. "Today we talk a lot about bullying, but back then, it was old-school prejudice. The same Daniel that is sitting here today smiling at you would come home crying as a kid. It happened many times; it wasn't just once.

"Going through that was extremely difficult for my parents and me, but that's where my parents showed great wisdom. They knew just how to talk to me. I understood that prejudice existed. It still exists, and it always will.

"The most important thing to remember about prejudice is that it can't exist within ourselves. I, with my disability, cannot think of myself as inferior. And the parents of a disabled child can't believe their child to be incapable of achieving something."

• • •

Before Daniel started school, he believed he was the only disabled person in his town. He grew up in a very small town, and while there were other disabled children living nearby, they never left the house. Daniel's parents, however, never kept him at home. He had a childhood just like every other kid — being sent outside to play, sometimes getting hurt, sometimes being grounded — all the normal things kids go through. He also had no siblings to compare himself to, so it took Daniel some time to notice that he was different.

Daniel is an only child not because his parents were worried about having another child with a disability, but because of the expense of supporting a child with unique needs. Today, Daniel has sponsorship that covers the cost of his prosthetics, but early on, his parents had to bear the huge financial burden themselves.

As a small child, Daniel went to AACD, a hospital in the city of São Paulo for children with special needs. That's when he started to notice that he was part of a larger community.

"I started to realize there were other people with disabilities," he says. "That's where I started to have contact with other disabled people, whether it was physical or intellectual. Before that, I had felt some sort of burden, thinking I was the only disabled person. I began to understand more about the universe of people with disabilities, and I realized I wasn't the only one. It liberated me in a sense, that I no longer carried that burden."

That understanding was just the tip of the iceberg. Ten years later, in 2004, the world of disability opened up even more to Daniel when he watched the Paralympics for the first time.

• • •

From his home in Camanducaia, sixteen-year-old Daniel watched in amazement as six thousand miles across the world in Athens, Greece, Clodoaldo Silva won his sixth gold medal at the 2004 Paralympic Games. Clodoaldo beamed as he sat proudly in his wheelchair, raising the Brazilian flag. Before that day, Daniel had never seen someone like himself compete on the world stage, and he had never had the opportunity to try swimming. His home town of Camanducaia in the state of Minas Gerais was very small, with just 20,000 people. Being deep in the countryside, it offered no exposure to swimming. To this day, there still isn't a swimming pool in the town.

As a kid, Daniel loved sports, and he believes that has made a huge difference to him — then and now. He says, "I believe in the power of sport to change a person's life. It really changed mine at age sixteen. I had always practiced sports, but I wasn't aware of swimming, especially Paralympic swimming."

After seeing Clodoaldo compete, Daniel had his mind set: he wanted to try swimming. He began taking a bus after school, riding for an hour and a half to the nearest pool in Bragança Paulista, practicing for an hour, and then getting back on the bus to go home for dinner.

Daniel proved to be an extremely fast learner. After just eight lessons, he was swimming all four strokes: freestyle, breaststroke, backstroke, and butterfly. He kept at it — making that long bus trip for the next two years, before moving to live closer to the pool.

"Clodoaldo was a huge role model, not only for the great athlete he was, but the great human being he is as well," says Daniel. "He's a fundamental part of the Paralympic Movement worldwide. If it wasn't for him, I wouldn't have been introduced to swimming, and perhaps Daniel Dias wouldn't have this wonderful story to share. He was the man who inspired me to swim, and even now, I tell him this is all his fault.

"In Brazil, we like to say we're the country of soccer. I don't think we are. I have to say that we're currently the country of Paralympic swimming."

• • •

From the moment Daniel entered that pool, he fell in love with swimming. He loved both the pain during practice and his daily focus on training. His goal? Simply to "seek to be better than I was yesterday, in every way of life."[1]

Daniel soon progressed to international competitions, first to the International Paralympic Committee Swimming World Championships in Durban, South Africa, in 2006, where he won three gold medals. Two years later, in 2008, twenty-year-old Daniel went to his first Paralympics, in Beijing, and he took home more medals than any other athlete — nine in total.

People were quick to compare Daniel to Michael Phelps, the American swimming phenom who won eight medals in Beijing. Whenever he was told he was the "Michael Phelps of the Paralympics," Daniel quickly countered with "No, I'm the Daniel Dias of the Paralympics."

"When I say I'm Daniel Dias and not Michael Phelps, first, I'd like to say that I'm extremely honored," says Daniel. "I know just what Phelps symbolizes not only to Americans but to the whole world. He's an exceptional man and an outstanding athlete, and being compared to a guy like that is a huge honor.

"But when I say 'I'm Daniel,' what I mean is that I'm advocating for an important flag, which is to represent the disabled. Through the sport, I have the chance to show the worth of a disabled person and, frankly, to eliminate that 'pity me' attitude. We don't want that. We just want to show everyone that we, even with our disability, want our space, want to conquer our own things.

"Through sport, I'm able to show people, including people with disabilities, what is possible. We need to fight and believe in our dreams. If you want to be a lawyer, then be the best one you can be. If you want to be a doctor, then be the best one you can be. I believe that today, through sport, I'm able to display those possibilities."

After Beijing, Daniel's swimming career continued at an impressive pace. He went on to compete in the London 2012 Paralympic Games, where he won another six gold medals. When the Paralympics came to his home turf in Brazil in 2016, he won another nine, including four gold. It was there, in Rio de Janeiro, that Daniel stepped onto the podium for the twenty-fourth time, becoming the greatest Paralympian in the world.

During each medal presentation in Rio, Daniel couldn't help but cry. Looking up into the stands, he could see his two-year-old son Asaph crying too. It meant everything to Daniel, making his son proud. As it turned out, Asaph wasn't crying out of pride, but out of possessiveness.

"After the end of the Games, I said to my wife, 'Wow, Asaph cried a lot, huh?' She said, 'Do you know why he cried? Because everyone was yelling 'Daniel, Daniel!' He cried saying, 'No, he is my daddy, not yours! Why are you calling his name?'"

• • •

Daniel first met his wife, Raquel, when he moved to Bragança Paulista in 2007 and began attending the same church she frequented. He remembers the day he first saw her: Raquel's bright blue eyes beaming as she walked in wearing a denim jacket. When they started talking, she had no idea about Daniel's athletic success, which he found endearing.

Unfortunately, at first, Raquel's parents disapproved of their relationship because of his disability, and the couple broke up. But a few years later, they reunited and decided to get married.

"We got married in 2012," says Daniel. "Back then, she couldn't care less if I was an athlete or not. She liked Daniel.

Daniel the person, Daniel the human being, Daniel the man. And then of course, after all of that, came Daniel the athlete. Above everything, she liked me for me. I thank God a lot for having her in my life. She is my support system."

Today, they have three children: Asaph, Daniel, and Hadassa. As an only child himself, Daniel says he always wanted his children to have siblings, and he's incredibly grateful for his family. Daniel hopes to teach his children a healthy mix of humility and compassion.

"I hope they understand we are all equal — that's the most important thing. We are all different in appearance, but in capability we are all the same, and that's what I try to show them. That they aren't inferior or superior to anyone. They can achieve things by believing in their potential, but never by belittling someone or putting someone down."

As a proud parent, Daniel often finds his children are the ones teaching him. The biggest lesson he's learned has come from his son Asaph. When he was six, Asaph told Daniel, "Dad, I want to be just like you." Proudly, Daniel jumped at the opportunity to share advice on how to become a successful athlete.

"I told him he's got to persevere. This life isn't easy, and he's got to train hard and be dedicated. He waited for me to finish and looked at me and said, 'Dad, I don't think you understand what I mean. I said that I want to be just like you. I don't want to have arms or legs.'

"Honestly, I couldn't even respond. The moment he said that I left the room and cried. He taught me such a big lesson that I had always carried with me but had never lived it so strongly before. He understood that what matters is the example you give.

"To him, it didn't matter if his dad had an arm or if he didn't: he wanted to be just like his dad in every way. And to me that's the true power of leading by example. And that's why I say, 'I'm Daniel Dias,' and I want to champion that. I think I'm on the right track, and my son Asaph showed me that. He taught me a major lesson."

• • •

Daniel is a role model for his fans as well as his children. He has been formally recognized by winning the Laureus Award for Sportsperson with a Disability three times. Often, after completing a training session, he is approached by children who watch him swim.

"Sometimes, when I get out of the water and look at the people sitting in the stands, I see children watching me. One time, a nondisabled child looked at me and said, 'Daniel, you're a role model to me.' And if I had thought about this when I first started, it would have seemed impossible. How does a person with a disability become a role model to someone without a disability? And that's what the sport has provided me. The kid was there looking at my willpower, my dedication, and not at the disability."

Daniel has a steadfast dedication to helping children. Several years ago, he launched the Daniel Dias Institute, a nonprofit that helps children with disabilities through sport and helps to create champions in life. Through the Institute, he's building a new fifty-meter pool that will support five thousand children, in the hopes of finding the next Daniel Dias. He's already helping one protégé: a young athlete named Andrey, one of the proudest success stories yet to come from the Institute.

"Andrey is one of those who looked up to me. He started swimming with us as a little boy, when he was nine. He's already twenty-four. He went to the Lima 2019 Parapan American Games and won a gold medal. We text each other frequently and I call him a younger brother. He's one of the people who has told me 'You were the source of my inspiration. I want to someday be where you are and achieve what you've achieved.'"

In reflecting on those achievements in sport, Daniel says there is just one more on his list: competing at the postponed Tokyo 2020 Paralympic Games. After that, he has his heart set on retirement — a decision that has been in the works for a long time.

"My decision to retire from sport is because of my family, thinking of my kids and how they grow up too fast. I want to cherish this time. I want to enjoy more time with them, be more present."

Daniel often gives advice to other parents, especially those who have a child with a disability.

"No parent expects to have a disabled child. When it happens, it's a huge shock for families and we need to help them. Most of the time the parents have no idea what to do — so what *do* they do? They keep their kids at home. The kids stay locked inside, hidden, don't go outside. The role of the Institute is to bring the kids out. And through sport, through swimming, the family understands that kids can have a normal life. They are different, but they can have a normal life: go to school, swim, run track, play soccer."

When Daniel talks with families, he hopes they can learn from his own experience and find purpose in life with disability. Daniel credits his parents, Paulo and Rosana, for their support and patience as Daniel found purpose in swimming.

And he recognizes the important role that Paralympian Clodoaldo Silva — who has cerebral palsy — played in showing Daniel what's possible. As Daniel said after competing in Rio in 2016, "I only began because I saw Clodoaldo swimming on television. I didn't know people like me could swim, could do any sport at all."[2]

He acknowledges that people don't always find their life purpose immediately, that it can take years.

"That's why you have to be patient, because there is no doubt your child will make you very proud one day. They will bring you infinite joy, just like every kid is an infinite joy in the eyes of their parents.

"Trust the purpose. Do not limit your child's potential. I can imagine what your heart must be like, how your head must be like. It can be very difficult, but everything in life has a purpose, I can say that from personal experience. Your child will surprise you one day.

"And don't forget to smile! Smile at life because things will get much easier. Smile for life!"

JUDY HEUMANN

It wasn't actually an "I," it was a "we."

Living in Washington, D.C., Judy is an
international disability rights advocate.
She contracted polio in childhood.

Brooklyn, New York, 1952

A fiercely intelligent five-year-old is denied entrance to school because of a few steps. The little girl in a wheelchair is considered a "fire hazard" by the principal, her chair a "dangerous obstruction."

Washington, D.C., 2010

Years later, that little girl, now a fiercely intelligent woman, is appointed by President Barack Obama as Special Advisor for International Disability Rights, a new position and one she would hold for his two terms in office.

One man sees a fire hazard, another sees a firebrand. One sees problems, another sees possibilities.

The story of disability rights activist Judy Heumann and the story of the U.S. disability movement are so interwoven one can't be told without telling the other. Here goes.

. . .

Judy was born in Brooklyn to German-Jewish immigrants. Judy's parents, Ilse and Werner, had come to live in the U.S. as teenagers in the 1930s, both having been sent separately to live with relatives.

Judy, the oldest of three children, contracted polio when she was eighteen months old, leaving her quadriplegic — unable to walk and with limited use of her hands and arms. She only discovered in her thirties that doctors had recommended she should be institutionalized. Though that was conventional advice at the time, it would never have been countenanced by her parents, themselves orphans of the holocaust. Instead, ignoring that advice, over the following years Judy's parents fought for her inclusion — a fight Judy herself would later take on.

After that day when Judy was turned away from kindergarten for being a fire hazard, her mother tried a local Jewish day school. The principal there said Judy could attend if she learned enough Hebrew, so Ilse arranged classes for Judy, only to have the principal later rescind the offer.

When Judy was six, the Board of Education contacted her mother to tell her that Judy was now eligible for home tuition, and she was granted two and a half hours per week. She has written of those days, "I did the meager homework . . . left for me, but what I mainly did was read. I read and read and read."[1]

Despite these early setbacks, Judy was included — and welcomed — in her neighborhood. She and the kids on her block figured out ways for her to participate in her wheelchair. That taught her at an early age that when you assume problems can be solved, most things are possible. She joined her siblings and friends for extracurricular activities such as Hebrew School, Scouts, and piano lessons. She also enjoyed robust discussion and debate around the family table.

It took much research, and it wasn't until Judy was nine years old, for her mother to succeed in finding a school Judy was allowed to attend — but it was an hour-and-a-half bus ride from home. The program, called Health Conservation 21, was specifically for disabled children. It was run out of the basement of a regular school, and very soon it became apparent to Judy that the two were different. The nondisabled kids (the children upstairs) were kept separate, got far more tuition time, were taught a regulated curriculum, and for them school was mandatory. She, on the other hand, had to take a nap and attend therapy, so daily tuition was less than three hours, and the students in her class ranged in age from nine to twenty-one.

While the program taught Judy little academically, she was happy to be able to get out of the house daily. As well, having the opportunity to talk with other disabled students about everything from dealing with people who stared to not being able to choose her own clothes (because her closet was inaccessible) to why they were being treated differently from the kids upstairs, she began to learn what could now be termed "disability culture."

Those early lessons would not be forgotten.

• • •

Her first taste of what life would be like if society truly included disabled people came from her summer camp experiences. From the time she started at Health Conservation 21 until she was eighteen, she attended camp.

It was there she first tasted freedom, and the experience was profound: "I went to two different camps over the course of my youth, and I would say both of them were very important because they were opportunities for me to be with other disabled people; to be learning how to spread my wings; to be learning what I was interested in and what barriers I felt I was facing, and we were facing as a group."

In her memoir, she has written of the significance of those summers:

Camp was . . . designed specifically with our needs in mind, and our parents paid for us to be a part of it. Our participation wasn't contingent on someone else's generosity; it was a given . . . The counselors were paid to do these things for us, which made all the difference in the world . . . asking people to do something for you when you're not paying them or they're not required to do it in some way means that you are asking someone for a favor.[2]

Many of the people Judy met at camp became lifelong friends and would also play important roles in the disability movement. (One of the camps she went to, Camp Jened, was featured in the 2020 Netflix documentary *Crip Camp*.)

• • •

Judy was the first person from her Health Conservation 21 program to go to high school, and that happened only because Ilse and some of the other mothers pressured the school district to make a number of schools in each borough wheelchair accessible.

However, it wasn't easy — getting to high school again involved a daily hour-and-a-half bus ride to and from home. As well, she was dependent on others at school, having to "ask for favors" to get from class to class or go to the bathroom.

She worked hard and was very successful academically. But exclusion remained a constant companion — for example, at her graduation ceremony, where she received an award, the stage was inaccessible to her, a wheelchair user.

Judy's parents encouraged her to go to college, despite neither of them having gone nor it being usual for females in the sixties to pursue higher education.

She was accepted to Long Island University. Although she wanted to become a teacher, to access funding to support her education, she had to study a course considered "acceptable" by the Office of Vocational Rehabilitation. Because of fixed views on what were realistic careers for disabled people, she studied speech therapy but took a minor in education to allow her to have enough credits to become a teacher.

Living on campus, Judy was again dependent on others for help. She grew close to other disabled students, and together they discussed many issues including wanting to make the university more accessible:

> We did not see our issue as a medical problem that, if we just "fixed" it, would be fine. We were beginning to see our lack of access as a problem with society, rather than our individual problem. From our perspective, disability was something that could happen to anyone at any time, and frequently did, so it was right for society to design its infrastructure and systems around this fact of life. We had grown up with the civil rights movement.[3]

Her campus activities fueled her confidence and she became more interested in politics. She ran for student council and won, and also got involved in the antiwar movement.

Once she finished college, Judy hit a major obstacle. She passed the oral and written exams for her teaching license but failed the medical. The reason given for her failing was that she couldn't walk, which in the opinion of the New York City Board of Education meant she was "a danger to children," and thus unable to teach.

Judy had to decide whether she would fight the board's decision. On one hand, she felt insecure and uncertain, but

ler, she felt a responsibility to fight not only for her-
r other disabled people. She says that was the first
vas faced with the decision to stand up for herself
for the right to do something.

She contacted the American Civil Liberties Union (ACLU)
for help, but they deemed there had been no discrimination.
Judy had no recourse as disability wasn't covered under the
Civil Rights Act of 1964, which addressed discrimination on
the basis of race, color, religion, and national origin — but
not disability. And at that time, there were no disability rights
organizations.

ACLU's response galvanized Judy into deciding to fight the
Board of Education — a daunting prospect.

Using her problem-solving skills learned from an early age,
Judy first strategized how to get publicity for the wrong. She
contacted a disabled friend, a journalism major, who helped
get an article and editorial published in *The New York Times*.
Two lawyers then volunteered to help fight the case. More
publicity followed, including one newspaper article with the
headline "You Can Be President, Not Teacher, with Polio"[4]
(alluding to Franklin D. Roosevelt, who used a wheelchair).

Judy has described that time as like a dam having broken.
She was energized by working with like-minded people who
recognized that, by working together, things can happen —
change can happen.

The case went ahead, and the New York City Board of
Education settled out of court. Judy was awarded her teaching license.

A teaching license isn't a teaching job, however. No school
would hire her, and many schools were still inaccessible. As
well, Judy suspected discrimination and the publicity surrounding the court case might be at play.

Eventually she got a job in her old school working with both the disabled and nondisabled kids. For the students it was the first time they had a teacher with a disability. Judy taught there for three years from 1970 to 1973.

...

Slowly, change was happening.

As a result of the court case, the State of New York passed legislation to allow blind people and people with a physical disability to become teachers.

Activism was also beginning.

In 1970, Judy and friends (including some from Camp Jened) formed a civil rights organization, initially called Handicapped in Action but soon after renamed Disabled in Action. Judy was its first president. Together they took on the fight for Section 504 of the Rehabilitation Act (the Rehab Bill).

Section 504 was one of the first pieces of federal legislation offering protection for people with disabilities. It applied to institutions receiving federal money such as transportation, hospitals, and education. President Nixon vetoed the legislation by allowing it to sit unsigned, arguing it would cost too much to implement. In response, in 1972, Disabled in Action organized a protest in New York to draw attention to this delay. One afternoon, about fifty people stopped the traffic on Madison Avenue and managed to shut down the city.

In 1973, Judy moved from New York to work at the Center for Independent Living in Berkeley, California. The novel center was run by disabled people for disabled people, to help them live independently. There, Judy herself got to experience "independent living" and flourished in her new life. She benefited from the financial support the State of California offered disabled people to hire personal assistants, meaning she wasn't dependent on roommates and friends as she had been in New York. While there, she completed a master's in public health at UC Berkeley.

Roughly a year later, Judy was on the move again, this time to Washington, D.C., to work as legislative assistant in Senator Harrison Williams's office. Williams was a champion of disability issues, and Judy got to work with the team on Section 504, as well as on what would eventually become the Individuals with Disabilities Education Act (IDEA). In 1975, Judy returned to Berkeley as deputy director of the Center for Independent Living, where she worked for seven years.

. . .

Eventually in 1973, President Nixon signed the Rehab Bill, including Section 504, but it still needed enabling regulations to be enforced. The Department of Health, Education, and Welfare (HEW) was responsible for drafting those. In 1974, Judy helped cofound the American Coalition of Citizens with Disabilities to track the progress of Section 504. The Coalition became the first national cross-disability rights organization run by and for people with disabilities.

During President Ford's administration, HEW drafted the enabling regulations and issued them for comment. Once institutions realized the implications of Section 504, particularly the cost, they organized for lobbyists to pressure the government. Delay ensued.

In 1977, Jimmy Carter, now president, promised that his HEW secretary, Joseph Califano, would sign the enabling regulations. Califano delayed again.

With the latest stall, the American Coalition of Citizens with Disabilities issued an ultimatum: if the regulations were not signed by April 5, 1977, there would be demonstrations across the country. That date came, the regulations were still unsigned, and demonstrations were held at HEW offices in ten U.S. cities.

Judy was in charge of planning the San Francisco demonstration. A protest was held outside the San Francisco Federal Building at 50 United Nations Plaza. Later that day, a large group of disabled people entered the building and went to the HEW office, which was on the fourth floor. There they began a sit-in that lasted almost a month.

Keeping the sit-in going involved massive organization — many of the disabled occupants had complex medical needs. Committees were formed to look after media, food, and medical and other supplies. Those inside were supported by the broader community outside who supported their fight for rights. When communications to the building were cut off, deaf people signed messages to the crowds outside.

Roughly halfway into the sit-in, a delegation from San Francisco, including Judy, went to Washington, D.C., where meetings, protests, and candlelight vigils were held. Judy and one other person remained in Washington until the regulations were signed, which eventually happened on April 28. Finally, disability had been redefined — from being regarded as a medical issue to being a question of civil and human rights.

• • •

After Section 504 was enforced, international visitors began coming to the Center for Independent Living — to learn about the work it was doing. Judy also traveled abroad to develop an understanding of the disability experience internationally. That led her, with two colleagues, to found the

World Institute on Disability in California. She worked there for ten years until 1993.

Meanwhile, domestic work continued. Section 504 covered only the public sector, and similar legislation was needed in the private sector. Over a number of years, legislation was developed, passed in the Senate, but got stuck in committees in the House of Representatives. In response, a protest was organized in Washington. Disabled people climbed the eighty-three steps to reach the Capitol's main entrance, by whatever means they could, some dragging themselves inch by inch.

Their action brought the delay into focus, and four months later the 1990 Americans with Disabilities Act (ADA) was signed into law, twenty-six years after the 1964 Civil Rights Act had passed. Finally, discrimination on the grounds of disability was now illegal in both the public and private sectors — people with disabilities were only now getting their civil rights.

• • •

In 1993, President Clinton appointed Judy as Assistant Secretary in the Office of Special Education and Rehabilitative Services in the Department of Education (OSERS). With a staff of about four hundred and a budget of $10 billion, she became the highest ranking disabled person in the U.S. government.

When President Clinton left office, Judy took up a role at the World Bank until she went to work for President Obama as Special Advisor for International Disability Rights. During his first term, Obama signed the United Nations Convention on the Rights for People with Disabilities. Though efforts were made to ratify this treaty, to date it still has not happened. Judy says, "I'm hopeful, but hopeful for when, I don't know."

Judy now works independently and remains very involved in many areas of international disability activism. She is a mentor to many, a public speaker much in demand (her 2016 TED Talk has been viewed over a million times), a networker, and a member of several boards, including CommunicationFIRST, a nonprofit to help those who cannot speak.

"I am not the retiring type, and there's still so much work to do," she says. "I enjoy what I'm doing, I enjoy meeting people. I enjoy being able to work on improving things which can benefit me and others. For me, this is never a job. I got engaged from the time I started experiencing discrimination, and since I and millions of other people still experience discrimination, I don't think about retiring."

She believes in the strength of using the media as a tool in disability. Recently, as a senior fellow at the Ford Foundation, she, together with Katherine Salinas and Michellie Hess, wrote the paper *Roadmap for Inclusion: Changing the Face of Disability in Media.*[5]

She says, "I think we're moving in the right direction, but there's a need for much greater representation of the voices of disabled people across the board in media. It's a combination of being able to 'see yourself,' but since so many disabilities are invisible, it's not the literal 'see yourself.' It's how the voices are represented — how people who have invisible disabilities feel comfortable and empowered by discussing their life — the barriers that they face, what they are doing to fight discrimination.

"Unless younger disabled people today are really looking at their media sources, they're less likely to know one or more disabled people, either personally, or through media."

Through *The Heumann Perspective* handle, Judy is attempting to "bring the voices of other disabled people forward in social media, and get people to have more understanding of the breadth of who disabled people are, as well as experiences of discrimination."

"I work right now with younger people — one is twenty-two and the other twenty-four — there's a really good connection between the three of us with our different skill sets. Both the others have hidden disabilities, which is very important for the work that we're doing."

Judy also pays a lot of attention to the disability movement across the lifespan.

"It's very important that we're looking at our movement more intergenerationally. It's important that we are supporting the voices of children, teenagers, and adults. It's important for people to understand that disability may be something they, or the people around them, may experience at some point.

"The community of people who are older and their family members don't necessarily look at issues like institutionalization, and what alternatives are there. They're not necessarily getting involved in discussions about legislation, community-based services and advocacy.

"For people who are acquiring disabilities, it's important to help them to continue to be the person they've been, to help them with the barriers they are experiencing."

• • •

The language of disability is very important too: words matter to Judy. She talks about using "disabled person" versus "person with disability," and "nondisabled" versus "able-bodied."

"I am a disabled person," she says. She does not describe herself or anyone else as a "person with disability."

She explains her rationale: "No other minority group puts the word 'person' or 'people' in front. No one says 'I'm a person who is a woman.' 'I'm a person who is Black.' 'I'm a person who is Jewish.' 'I'm a person who is LGBT.'

"People-first language originated with disabled people with intellectual disabilities saying that they wanted to be treated like they're a person, because many people were living in institutions, getting terrible treatment, and being dehumanized.

"I believe it was the nondisabled professionals who were really pushing for that terminology.

"For me, I use the term 'disabled people.' Others use 'people with disabilities' — that's their choice, but I will frequently talk with them and ask why.

"Some people go 'whatever.' I've never bought into the 'whatever.'"

She also adds: "I'm not a disabled person with a capital 'A' [disAbled]. I'm not a disabled person crossing out the 'dis' [~~dis~~abled]."

Judy also uses the term "nondisabled," rather than "able-bodied."

"The connotation of the word 'able,' [in 'able-bodied'] implies that I'm not. I would argue that 'able-bodied' is not a neutral term.

"Saying 'nondisabled' suggests to people that at some point in their lives, they may have a temporary or permanent disability — they don't get an opt-out card. They don't get to say 'I'm able and you're not.'

"People aren't necessarily using those terms in a pejorative way, but for me, as someone who has a disability, those terms make me feel like there is a power dynamic that I don't like or want.

"The movement is really about our being able to become full members of our society, and so I think words matter."

...

Through it all, Judy has found time for other interests and a home life with her husband. She married Jorge in 1992: "He likes what I do; he believes in what I do. At the same time he frequently complains that I work too much. But he's definitely proud of what I do."

More recently, she wrote her memoir, *Being Heumann*, with Kristen Joiner, which was published in 2020. In its opening, Judy explains that any story of changing the world is always the story of many — "It wasn't actually an 'I,' it was a 'we.'"[6]

One saw a fire hazard, another saw a firebrand. Judy Heumann certainly helped light the fire that became a movement — the U.S. disability movement — that helped to advance disability rights across the world.

JESSICA LONG

Be so good they can't ignore you

Jessica is a U.S. Paralympic swimmer who was adopted as a young child from Russia. She is an amputee as a result of fibular hemimelia.

FLOATING IN AN EXPANSE of shimmering water, Jessica Long extends her arms out wide, rotating them upward as she places goggles over her eyes. The camera pans out to show Jessica kicking calmly, revealing her legs, both of which have been amputated below the knee. Jessica wears a gray swim cap and a red swimsuit, red being a national color in both her birth country of Russia and her adopted home, the United States.

That emblematic shade of red is also the brand color for Toyota, Jessica's sponsor and the advertiser featuring Jessica in the iconic 2021 Super Bowl commercial. The minute-long film tells Jessica's story, interweaving shots of Jessica as a baby and young girl with scenes of her as an adult — displaying her journey from adoption to success as a Paralympic swimmer for Team USA.

For Jessica, that commercial was a very moving moment in a successful career, which started at age twelve when she made her international debut at the Athens 2004 Paralympic Games, becoming the youngest member of the U.S. Paralympic Team. She has since gone on to win twenty-three medals at four Paralympic Games, becoming one of the most successful Paralympians of all time.

She acknowledges the attention she's received since the airing of the ad: "There were so many things in that commercial that were powerful. I have had this wild journey, and I never would have pictured that it would have ended up in a Super Bowl commercial for everyone to see. It was very raw, and real.

"I want people to be inspired. I have always wanted to be an inspiration to people, but I don't want to be inspiring for getting a cup of coffee or going to the grocery store. That's just everyday life — those are things I do because I adapt, and humans are amazing at adapting to anything. Instead, I want people to be inspired by my accomplishments and hard work, because my success is twenty years in the making. It hasn't happened overnight."

Adopted from an orphanage in Siberia at thirteen months, Jessica was brought home to Baltimore, Maryland, by her new parents, Steven and Beth Long. Her parents were aware at the time of her adoption that Jessica had fibular hemimelia and would require surgery to amputate her legs.

Growing up, Jessica took advantage of every opportunity she had, thanks to the support of her adoptive parents.

• • •

Jessica was born in Bratsk, Russia, in 1992, as Tatiana Olegovna Kirillova. Her teenage mother placed her in an orphanage, a decision she later told Jessica was meant to be temporary until she could return a few years later to bring Jessica home. At the time of Jessica's birth in Russia, Steven and Beth, her adoptive parents in the U.S., were facing secondary infertility. They had two children already but struggled to get pregnant again, and they had always dreamed of having four children.

After trying for eight years, they decided to pursue adoption, and it took a mere three months to complete the process, confirming their decision as soon as they saw photos of Jessica and her brother, Josh. Both were in the same

Russian orphanage and both had a disability — Jessica with fibular hemimelia, and Josh, a cleft lip and palate. With two other children at home, Beth opted to stay in Maryland while Steven took his first trip out of the country to Russia to bring Jessica and Josh home.[1]

"I feel like I won the lottery when it came to parents, because there was so much love — adopting two kids with special needs," says Jessica.

Amazingly, shortly after Jessica and Josh arrived in the U.S., Beth got pregnant again — not once, but twice, with Jessica's two younger sisters, completing the Long family with six children.

Growing up in Baltimore, Jessica was raised in a warm, happy household, and with a childhood marked by a series of early surgeries. She had her first operation, to amputate both her legs, when she was eighteen months old, and continued to have surgeries every couple of months. She remembers those formative years as a time that taught her the power of determination.

"I realize how tough and loving my parents were," says Jessica. "They truly loved all of me."

Jessica's parents were devoted to their family. Beth home-schooled all six children, while Steven worked outside the home. Every night the Long family gathered together for dinner. Steven made family time a priority and was the one to tuck in the kids every night at bedtime. That routine established a very close bond between Jessica and her dad.

"I've always had a really special connection with my dad," says Jessica. "As I've gotten older, I've learned that maybe that connection comes from being adopted. My birth mom gave me up, and I would often butt heads with my adoptive mom.

My dad was the one that really got me, which is common. As a result of adoption, a lot of girls are really close to their dads."

Steven was also the one who encouraged Jessica's interest in swimming early on. Every Sunday, Jessica and her family spent the afternoon at her grandparents' house, eating lunch together after church and, when the weather was good, swimming in their backyard pool.[1] Jessica was happiest in the water, and she quickly fell in love with swimming.

When Jessica was ten, her grandmother encouraged her to join a local swim team. Jessica relished in perfecting new strokes and discovered she was strong and fast — faster than many of her nondisabled friends. She has said of swimming that "all my life I have had to fight to catch up with people. But not in the water. That's the one place where everyone else is trying to keep up with me!"[2]

"A lot of my success came from parents who let me do my own thing," says Jessica. "It was always my decision to be a swimmer. I never grew up with parents who lived through me. They're very proud of me but they care more about having good character. My parents allowed me to dream big and challenge myself, where nothing was ever out of reach."

At age eleven, Jessica learned about the Paralympic Games and set an ambitious goal for herself: to qualify for the U.S. Paralympic Team competing in Athens the following year.

• • •

Twelve-year-old Jessica steps up to the podium, wearing a red, white, and blue zip-up jacket. A gold medal is placed around her neck and she's presented with a bouquet of flowers and the Greek *kotinos* wreath that adorns the head of every medalist. Jessica is the youngest member of the U.S. delegation at these Athens 2004 Paralympic Games, and the winner of three gold medals.

"What motivated me was that little girl who fell in love with swimming and never looked back. I started because it gave me a sense of feeling strong and feeling capable," says Jessica. "Being tough and determined was also a coping mechanism, a kind of survival when you're a little kid."

After those first Games in 2004, Jessica's career took off. In 2006, she won nine gold medals at the International Paralympic Committee's (IPC's) Swimming World Championships, the same year she was named the top amateur athlete in the country when she won the James E. Sullivan Award and was named U.S. Paralympian of the Year. At the Beijing 2008 Games, she earned six Paralympic medals and broke three world records. She followed that with eight medals in London 2012 and six medals in Rio 2016. At every Games, she followed comedian Steve Martin's dictum to "be so good they can't ignore you."

"I want people to remember me as a professional elite athlete. It's years and years of hard work. It's one thing to get to the top and it's another thing to stay at the top. I'm really proud that I'm still a part of the sport," says Jessica. "I would love to end my career at the Los Angeles 2028 Paralympic Games. It would be my seventh Paralympics. I've been waiting my whole life for the Games to come to the United States, so what better way to end my career?"

Reflecting on disability and the Paralympic Games, Jessica says she sees an opportunity to push for even more progress. "It's interesting to me here in the U.S., where we are all about being your own person — being unique and different and promoting body positivity — but there's still so much lacking in acceptance of disability and adapting to disability. There's still a little bit of shame there. I would love it to be where people don't even question what the Paralympics are."

Jessica is thrilled that the coverage of the Paralympics has grown over the course of her seventeen-year swimming career. She notices that people are even starting to pronounce the event correctly, saying "Paralympics" instead of "Para-Olympics." Despite the progress made, however, there are still areas where she hopes to see change — and to be part of that change. Having won the ESPY Award (the sports equivalent of the Oscars for film or Tonys for theater) for Best Female Athlete with a Disability three times, she questions why she is in a separate category.

"I struggle with some of the awards I've won," says Jessica. "I ask, 'Why are we not in the same category as all athletes? Why do we have to be separate?' I would love to change the dynamic of awards."

• • •

The U.S. Olympic & Paralympic Committee is making great progress toward parity between Olympic and Paralympic athletes. In 2018, the committee voted to equalize payments for Olympians and Paralympians, so that all athletes now earn the same bonus for winning a medal at the Games.[3] That change in bonus structure reflects the work and dedication each athlete puts into elite sport and shows that the value of all athletes is equal. This was a very positive and welcomed move, representing a four- to fivefold increase in earning potential for Paralympic athletes.[4,5]

While this progress toward parity is great, Jessica fears it may create an extra incentive among Paralympians to win at all costs.

As Jessica and some other para athletes see it, the classification system is one of the issues. As explained by the IPC, "Classification is the cornerstone of the Paralympic Movement; it determines which athletes are eligible to compete in a sport and how athletes are grouped together for competition."[6] In swimming, "there are ten different sport classes for athletes with physical impairment, numbered 1-10. The lower the number, the more severe the activity limitation. Athletes with different impairments compete against each other, because sport classes are allocated based on the impact the impairment has on swimming, rather than on the impairment itself. To evaluate the impact of impairments on swimming, classifiers assess all functional body structures using a point system and ask the athlete to complete a water assessment."[7]

Jessica acknowledges that officials aim to create a fair system but that many would agree that there are a number of challenges within it.

"When I was in Germany in 2016, one of the girls told me she was going to cheat. She was telling me she's going to swim slower for her review swim. I asked, 'What do you mean?' It didn't even cross my mind that people did that." Jessica has also heard athletes in the locker room saying to each other, "I'm in the wrong [easier] class," which she finds heartbreaking.

"I think we need surprise classifications, just like we get surprise drug testing," she says.

Another challenge Jessica sees is that as an amputee, her disability is very clear while others are less so and require a level of interpretation. She cites the example of the Irish swimmer Ailbhe Kelly, who recently retired at age twenty because of challenges with the classification system.[8]

Jessica hopes to help make the system better for everyone. Paralympic swimming is increasing in popularity, and she acknowledges that she shares the same goals as the officials: to bring more people into the sport and grow the Movement.

"I have poured my entire life into the Paralympics, and I know the power of the Paralympic Movement. It gave me confidence: this little girl who didn't want to show her legs. It changed my life. I know how it can change the lives of other little girls and boys.

"My goal is first to ask, 'How do we make the system better?' and then to help pave the way, just like others before me."

• • •

As she does with her sport, Jessica hopes to use her influence to bring attention to adoption. Despite being raised in an environment where her adoptive parents gave her unconditional love, Jessica still has feelings of pain and anger, feelings she believes that people considering adoption should be aware of.

"I want people to know that adoption is really hard. It's a process. It's such a beautiful thing, but it's also a real tragedy, what happens to these babies. That abandonment is something that doesn't just go away. There was so much love in my family, but as I've gotten older, I've felt a lot of anger. Anger was a very comfortable emotion for me; it was very easy to be angry. It's hard, because I was always told, 'You were the child meant for us.' I want parents to be patient, and to understand that it is a process for the child.

"I can see the amount of selfless love that goes into adoption, and I do think it's worth it. But you have to be prepared for some real tough moments."

At times, Jessica didn't want to tell her parents how she was feeling. "As a little kid, you just think all these crazy thoughts.

My birthday is on February 29, and I used to think that I was nonexistent in the world because I didn't have a birthday every year. Now that I'm older, I've shared those things with my mom, and she can't even believe that I thought this. My birthday is a hard day, because it's the day I was born into this world, but it's also the day I was given up."

After Jessica rose to fame competing in London in 2012, Russian reporters tracked down her biological parents, who had watched Jessica swim without realizing she was their daughter. In 2013, ahead of the Paralympic Winter Games in Sochi, executives at NBC, the American broadcaster for the Games, organized a trip for Jessica to return to Russia and meet her biological parents. That's when she learned that her birth mother, a teenager at the time of Jessica's birth, was encouraged by doctors to give up her baby, even though she didn't want to.

When the reunion aired on NBC in 2014, Jessica spoke about her mother, saying, "I think that was really brave, and I don't know what I would have done if I was in her situation, at sixteen and having this disabled baby that they knew that they couldn't take care of . . . I have so much love for her, my mom, because she gave me life."[9] Over the last five years, Jessica has been in therapy, a process she has found to be healing.

In 2015, Jessica began training with legendary coach Bob Bowman in her hometown of Baltimore, Maryland. Just two years later, in 2017, she met her husband, Lucas. At that time, she was getting up at 5:30 a.m. to train alongside Olympic swimmers and going to bed at 7:30 p.m. She had no intention of getting distracted by boys, but she fell in love. They married in October 2019.

"He is my best friend, and I think that's the most important thing, to have that foundation of friendship," says Jessica.

"He's totally different from me: he's just go-with-the-flow patient, and really easygoing."

• • •

In the lead-up to the Tokyo Games, Jessica is back in Colorado Springs at the Olympic and Paralympic Training Center (OPTC) for several months, while Lucas is home in Maryland. She's able to focus on training and sleep, and take advantage of the resources at the OPTC, like catered food and on-site physical therapy.

When the Games were originally postponed, in March of 2020, Jessica felt a sense of relief. She had spent the last year and a half focused on planning her wedding and enjoying being a newlywed — life was full of transitions, so she appreciated the opportunity to relax a bit.

"I'm very grateful to have had an extra year. It gave me a chance to spend time with my husband. I got to decide that I still love swimming and want to be a part of it. After eighteen years of swimming, you always have to find new inspiration and excitement.

"When the postponement happened, I was out of the water for seventy-five days. I still went on the rowing machine and bike, trying to be as consistent as possible. I knew that was something I was really good at: being mentally tough. I know how to adapt and put my full focus on something even when things don't go perfectly.

"I think good things come to those who work really, really hard. I've seen that in my life, and I'm really happy to still be part of the sport. I'm a smarter swimmer now. I have the yardage and the experience. Things are coming back to me and I'm gaining that confidence again."

Jessica is training harder than she's trained in years. She hopes that her journey can serve as an inspiration to others.

"I want people to be inspired by that little girl, to see where I came from," says Jessica. "There were moments of struggles and moments of doubts, feeling insecure that no one would ever like me because I'm the girl with no legs. But then, if you think about it, me — the girl with no legs — just had a Super Bowl commercial. It's wild."

ILA ECKHOFF

It's what I can do that matters

Ila is a managing director at BlackRock's
New York office and has cerebral palsy.

Mother's Day, 2014

Dear Mom,

It's hard to put into words how much you really mean to me
. . . You are by far the most inspiring person I've ever met.
Having the confidence and strength you possess on a daily
basis is something that I will always revere. One of your most
admirable traits is your unwillingness to give up, which is
demonstrated in everything you do. I will never properly be
able to commend you for what you've done for me or even
begin to explain the impact you've had on my life, but I will
never stop trying. I love you. Happy Mother's Day!

Love, Peri

The extract from a thank-you letter written by Ila Eckhoff's
daughter Peri, then aged seventeen, is one of several published
for Mother's Day by the New York daily paper *Newsday*.[1] Peri
wrote the letter shortly after Peri's dad — Ila's husband —
died from complications following an accident.

Ila Eckhoff, mom and step-mom, is a managing director
and senior member of the global investment operations team
at BlackRock. A Fortune 500 company, BlackRock is the
world's largest asset management company. Working for the

past 20 years at their New York office, Ila also represents the company on various industry forums and advisory committees. Ila has cerebral palsy.

...

Going back to the start, Ila recounts, "I was born two-and-a-half months premature and weighed 3 lbs. 6 oz. My mother hemorrhaged all the way to the hospital, and I spent significant time in an incubator." Both Ila and her mother were given only a fifty-fifty chance of making it. "My mom said that my head fit in one hand and the rest of my body in the other."

Her mom also told her that she "screamed louder than any other kid in the nursery, so they had to feed me first. They knew I was going to survive because making such loud noise meant that I was getting enough oxygen."

Ila was diagnosed with cerebral palsy when she was two. It mostly affects her lower limbs, and today she walks using a cane for balance.

Between the ages of two and sixteen, Ila had twelve surgical procedures. The repeated message surgeons gave her parents was that if they didn't operate she may not be able to walk — so her parents always agreed. Ila describes those surgeries as a nightmare, and she has particularly bad memories of one surgeon: "I was the guinea pig, and Murphy's Law and I got along really well. I spent one year in four different body casts."

Signs of the strong adult Ila would become were evident early. Having happily changed surgeons around age fourteen, Ila made things clear from the start: "There's no surgery that you do on me that you don't discuss with me first. Any decisions that need to be made, we make together. As good as you are, I'm sure there's another guy down the hall, who's just as good. These are my rules of engagement."

Her harsh encounters with the medical system were not just a feature of her childhood in the sixties and seventies; they continued into adulthood — for example, doctors who couldn't do a pap smear for a woman with cerebral palsy, or who questioned why a woman with cerebral palsy would even need birth control. She believes that this displays a complete lack of understanding and empathy, and that change is still needed.

Ila's father supported and encouraged his determined, young daughter; after all, like father like daughter.

When she was just five, her dad laid it on the line: "You're going to have to be better, smarter, and faster to be thought of as an equal. The sooner you accept that and move on, the better off you're going to be because you can't change it." To drive home his point, he took her at that young age to an institution for children with severe developmental disabilities to shock her into realizing that she could have had a much more profound disability had her birth been delayed by just another five minutes. He added that he never, ever wanted to see her feeling sorry for herself.

It was tough love. Ila got the message.

Ila says, "The desire to be the best or to truly believe that I could do anything I set my mind to comes from my dad. When I was growing up, if the doctor said, 'We're going to do this operation and it's going to take you six months to a year to walk, after we do it,' my dad would look at me and say, 'What do you say we do it in three months?'"[2] Ila would answer, "Okay," and they would set the goal and go from there. They didn't necessarily make the goal, but setting it was just an extra push.

"My parents really believed that I could do anything. All I had to do was decide that I wanted to do it, but I had to believe it, and I think the way children internalize belief is that parents have to believe it first. You have to give that, in a sense, like a gift to your child. So I do the same thing with my daughter. She knows I expect great things from her, but I believe in the power that she brings to everything she does.[2]

"At one point because of surgeries, I missed over two years of school but ultimately came back ahead of my classmates.

"I graduated high school on time, went to college, graduate school, and obtained an MBA/CPA. Each success has driven me to a rewarding thirty-plus year career in financial services."[3]

Ila remembers, "I knew from the time I could talk to my parents that I would be going to college. And originally, I wanted to be a doctor, but organic chemistry and I didn't get along very well. So after a semester in college and hating chemistry more than I thought I could hate anything on Earth, I changed my major to economics."[2]

Ila lost her mom to cancer and heart failure when she was just eleven years old. She says, "I have had more than my share of hardship, and yet, I am grateful to be where I am today. All of the earlier struggles and losses brought me here, now. Without them the outcome would be different. Resiliency is not about how you bounce back from a single, even traumatic event; it is how you respond every day to the challenges that life presents. Repetitive use of this 'muscle' builds strength, enables you to do more — and sometimes the impossible."[4]

• • •

Today, as a senior executive in financial services, Ila has much to say about disability in the workplace and how her thinking has changed over the years. She says, "When you have a disability, you want people to accept you as you. You don't want to be accepted because 'it's Ila Eckhoff who has cerebral palsy.' It's 'I want to be accepted for who I am.' So I spent my entire life trying to make my disability disappear, meaning I had to be better, smarter, faster. When people see me when I walk in the door with a cane and a gait that's different from everybody else's, I know they're making certain judgments whether they want to or not. So if I want to be looked at as an equal, I have to be better.[2]

"I also sit on the board of the Cerebral Palsy Foundation.[5] Until I did that, I didn't self-disclose [about having a disability]. I used to go into job interviews and put the cane under the desk. I would try to get there early enough so I could hide it somewhere and find a chair to sit down so when I did my interview, it wasn't even a discussion. They couldn't see it until I left. Which gave me an opportunity first. Thank God it's not the sixties, seventies, and eighties anymore and the world has gotten better."[6]

As for the importance of employment for people with disabilities, Ila says, "Everyone is born with gifts to bring the world and everyone deserves to work, deserves a chance to prove oneself . . . Employment matters for people with disabilities for more than just financial reasons. Employment matters because people with disabilities are seeking the opportunity to achieve independence, just like anyone else. We also want to fulfill our dreams, we want to get married, we want to have families, and we have the same aspirations as those without disabilities.

"Some states have deliberate strategies implemented by leaders in the community, in government and in the school system that place a priority on 'Employment First.' This is a strategy where critical social programs are oriented toward ensuring that getting a job is the top priority for individuals with disabilities. That goal is reinforced with high expectations among the teachers, coaches, and parents for that individual."[4]

These strategies, she says, don't just benefit people living with the disabilities; they offer tangible benefits to the organizations that hire them. "Companies that embrace employees with disabilities clearly see the results in their bottom line. [They] have higher productivity levels and lower staff turnover rates, are twice as likely to outperform their peers in shareholder returns and create larger returns on investment.

"The fact is that disability is part of the human experience. It is nothing to fear because most of us will be affected by it eventually, whether by accident, aging, or illness. Diverse teams make better decisions. People with disabilities often excel in social and emotional competence skills — people management, coordination/collaboration with others, emotional intelligence, judgment and decision making, service orientation, and negotiation. Opening more job opportunities to people with disabilities will mean stronger communities and a better economy for all. Achieving that requires all of us working together because people with disabilities are the right talent, right now."[4]

Four years ago BlackRock launched an Ability Network, adding to their other employee networks created to support their personnel's diverse experiences and backgrounds. The Ability Network had Ila's strong support from day one. "Why ability? It's because I'm sick and tired of talking about all the things that people with disabilities can't do. The dialogue needs to change. The language needs to change. It's about what we *can* do. And we illustrate that by example. We illustrate that by pushing forward. So I mentor young people both at my firm and throughout the industry. I am always looking for different opportunities to connect with people so that they understand. We have to tell our story."[6]

Ila assists the diversity, equity, and inclusion team at work. She believes she has a lot to offer, as a female, as an older person, as a person with a disability, and because, as she says, "I'm not exactly shy." Ila loves this work — it's work that she is doing more and more of both within and outside the company. She is in demand in this space. This is work that she will continue to do when she eventually retires.

. . .

Ila has given a lot of thought on many aspects of disability, ranging from parenting a child with a disability to role models and more.

On the topic of parenting, she says, "The problem with a lot of parents that have kids with cerebral palsy is that they cater to them. 'Oh, they can't do that. Oh, you're asking too much.'

"The best advice I could give any parent of a kid with a disability is not allow them to use that as an excuse for anything. We all have things we're good at and things we're not — whether you have a disability or not. For those with disabilities the challenges can be more obvious — my challenge is visible. The thing that everybody has to do is figure out what they're good at and what they're not; focus on what they're good at."

When she was young, there were no role models with disability. Today, that's beginning to change: "Look at film and television shows like *Speechless*, and *The Good Doctor* that give people with disabilities somebody to look up to."[6]

It was her father who trained her how to deal with bullying as a child in school. "I would go to school and kids would steal my crutches; kids would trip me going down the stairs, because they thought that was funny to watch the girl with cerebral palsy fall down the stairs. 'It's not funny.'"

As for her friends, she says, "They are my 'framily' — friends that I treat like family."

"Framily" was the moat that Ila built around herself. They protected her. This moat "gave me the space to then build my confidence, try new things, take risks," she says. "I would do *anything* for those friends."

• • •

On her road through life, Ila has learned a lot through failure. Remembering the time she changed her major in college, she says, "That wasn't the first time I experienced failure. I have learned much more from failure than from success. So I embrace failure now, I actually kind of look for it. Because those challenges that I then overcome make me better, stronger, and faster for the next thing. Resilience is something you have to build. It doesn't happen overnight. It's not one incident that teaches you resilience, it's a full life experience."[6]

Of grit, she has this to say: "Grit is kind of like my middle name. I do think it's really important. Grit is one of those things that we don't quite know how to measure. Grit has been proven to have much more of an impact on goals, objectives, and achievement — even more than intellect. Granted, you need an education; you need to be able to talk; where you come from is also important. But a person with above-average grit is going to go a lot further than somebody who's super smart with zero grit who, once they get stopped, doesn't know how to get back up."

Learning from failure, building resilience, embodying grit — it all adds up to self-advocacy, a big part of Ila's message, for everyone — with or without a disability. "You're responsible for your life. Nobody else is. Don't wait for somebody else to take care of it, for somebody else to fix it. You're responsible."

Today, Ila feels she's "pretty much unstoppable now." She says, "I look at my disability as kind of my superpower, not as my impediment. But it's taken me a long time to get here. When I was younger, trust me, cerebral palsy was not my superpower. It was a royal pain in the ass."

But now she doesn't look at herself as somebody with disability. "I am a strong and capable woman who happens to have cerebral palsy. I am not cerebral palsy."

In short, Ila Eckhoff's key message is this: "It's what I *can* do that matters."[2] And she continues to do a lot that matters.

CHANTAL PETITCLERC

Diversity is not just our signature, it is our strength, and we must never forget it.

Chantal is a Canadian senator and retired Paralympic wheelchair racer. She became paralyzed as a result of an accident in adolescence.

FRENCH-SPEAKING QUEBEC is Canada's largest province by area and second by population in Canada. It lies east of Ontario and Hudson Bay. Saint-Marc-des-Carrières, a small town of roughly 3,000 people in the south of the province, sits close to the Saint Lawrence River. "Carrière" is the French word for "quarry" — the town being named after the nearby limestone quarries.

Chantal Petitclerc was born in Saint-Marc-des-Carrières in 1969, the oldest of three children born to Georges, a building contractor, and Céline, a homemaker. When Chantal was thirteen years old, a heavy barn door fell on her in an accident at a neighbor's farm, causing a spinal injury. Chantal became paraplegic, losing the use of her legs.

Fast forward to 2021. Chantal is serving as an independent member in the Canadian Senate, the country's Upper House of Parliament. The House was debating a bill on medical assistance in dying (the MAID bill), a contentious piece of legislation for many, who asserted that the proposed bill discriminated against people with disabilities. During the debate, Chantal, who supported the bill, spoke of her personal experience with disability:

> This coming summer, it will be 38 years since the day I had my accident. The study of this bill keeps bringing me back

to the little girl that I was, lying on the ground, unable to feel my legs and unable to get up. I knew from that moment that my life would never be the same again and that I would need to adjust to that new reality very quickly. It reminds me of my mom, just divorced a year before my accident, a low-wage worker with three kids, my little brother not even two years old, me in a wheelchair, and her having to carry me up and down to the second floor of our apartment building because we could not afford to move. I may be privileged to be here in the Senate of Canada, but I never forget where I came from, and I know exactly what it is to be in a situation of extreme vulnerability.[1]

Chantal's argument was that rather than discriminate, the bill empowered people — all people — giving them choice and "striking a balance between protecting the vulnerable and respecting the autonomy of individuals to seek medical help to end intolerable suffering."[2]

. . .

Chantal says she always finds it a bit strange when people ask her about her accident, because she doesn't have that many memories of it. It wasn't a moment of great despair for her. "I recall it as being, for sure, a life-changing event and challenging and adapting to this new reality, the new abilities that you have, the new limits that you have. But also, how you view yourself as a young girl, how you suddenly become someone with a difference, and how that has an impact because you don't choose to be that new person with a difference, and especially not in a small town.

"You become a person with a disability, but when it happens at the age of thirteen, it is a bit of a strange time because you are undergoing so many changes already in terms of defining who you are as a young girl and how you relate to others.

"At that time, there were fewer role models or known persons with disability, so I guess it was a very isolating time."

It helped Chantal that the townspeople and her school rallied to support her. She says, "I guess maybe one of the strengths of a small town is that everybody knows each other. I was very lucky, because I had my teachers and some amazing people in the school. I was very lucky that school was a bit of a comfort place and a positive environment for me."

One of the individuals who supported her was a physical education teacher, Gaston Jacques, who taught her to swim. "I started swimming and that was really important. At the time, they simply didn't quite know what to do for a person with a disability — there weren't programs or legislation either. I was quite lucky that my teacher did it without any programs. I started swimming during lunchtime, and I did that for five years."

When Chantal was eighteen, she watched the Paralympic Games for the first time, which would prove to be very influential for her. "The Seoul Games was the first time that the Olympics and the Paralympics were held in the same facilities. That year there were some very strong and well-known Canadians participating," she says.

"They really were my first role models because we didn't know of the Paralympic Movement; we didn't know anybody who was a person with a disability. They weren't on TV or in advertising, so I was very inspired by the Paralympians and that's how I took up wheelchair racing when I moved from my small town to college in Quebec City."

While Chantal was studying social sciences at the CEGEP (a pre-university college system in Quebec) in Quebec City, she was introduced to wheelchair racing by Pierre Pomerleau, a trainer at Université Laval. It was a sport that soon took over from swimming for her. "Wheelchair racing and wheelchair basketball were the two adapted sports that were best known. I wanted to be with a group. In the beginning, it wasn't about being competitive — it was about being in an organized sport."

In those early days of her racing, her racing chair was homemade. New racing chairs at the time would put an athlete back about $4,000, which Chantal couldn't afford, so with $400 from her father, she had one cobbled together from other used racing chairs. Chantal joined the national wheelchair racing team in 1988 when she was nineteen years old.

In 1991, Chantal went to the University of Alberta in Edmonton and studied history. There she trained with Peter Eriksson, who became and remained her coach throughout her career.

• • •

In 1992, as a class T54 wheelchair racer, Chantal competed in her first Paralympics in Barcelona, winning two medals. She went on to win medals at all five Paralympic Games in which she competed, starting with Barcelona, then Atlanta 1996, Sydney 2000, Athens 2004, and finally Beijing 2008. In total, she has won twenty-one Paralympic medals in distances from 100 to 1500 meters. Over the years, she set many world records, and to this day she still holds the 200 meter record, set in Beijing.

She also won medals at World Championships and Commonwealth Games, and was honored to be the flagbearer for the Canadian team at the 2006 Commonwealth Games.

Over those competitions, one very special moment came at her final race, in her final Paralympics.

Just before she left for training camp prior to going to Beijing, she spent some precious time with her grandfather, who was dying. Leaving him was very difficult, and he passed away soon after. She remembers, "Those Games were very unique, and the pressure was on more than ever before in my life. The team really wanted to win those five gold medals.

"It was the final race, and it was raining, which was the one thing I didn't want. There was a lot of pressure, but also a lot of adrenaline and excitement, and this out-of-control rain was playing with my head. Everyone was in a panic because of the rain, so I went away to find some space.

"Sometimes you're in the moment. The one thought that came to me was my grandfather telling me that I could do it.

"Everything is a mindset. It just kind of switched my mindset — not to be sure that I was going to win, but to be sure that I was going to fight for it. If I was going to lose this race, it was not going to be in my head. Maybe I would lose because of slipping. Maybe I would lose because someone would be faster, but I certainly was not going to lose because of my mindset and being scared. That gave me the strength to want to fight for it.

"I wanted to do that for my grandfather. It was a very special moment."

That's what athletes can do, she says: dig deep and find what they need.

• • •

Chantal retired from the sport following the Beijing 2008 Paralympic Games, and in the years following she became involved in team management. She worked with the British wheelchair racing team for the 2012 London Paralympics alongside her former coach Peter Eriksson, who was by then Paralympic head coach for UK Athletics. She was named chef de mission for the Canadian team for both the 2014 Commonwealth Games team and 2016 Paralympic Games in Rio de Janeiro.

Over the years, Chantal's sporting achievements have been recognized with many awards. In 2008 she won the Lou Marsh Trophy, presented annually to Canada's top athlete. That year she also won the Bobbie Rosenfeld Award for Female Athlete of the Year, as judged by The Canadian Press. In 2009, she won Best Female Athlete at the Paralympic Sport Awards, and she was also inducted into Canada's Walk of Fame in Toronto.

There was one award that Chantal turned down — the 2004 Jack W. Davies Trophy for Outstanding Canadian Athlete of the Year in Athletics (track and field). She refused it on a matter of principle — because she was named cowinner with Olympic hurdler Perdita Felicien, who had failed to win a medal in Athens, the same Games where Chantal had won five gold medals and set three world records.[3]

Chantal remembers this as a very difficult time. While she had quietly turned down the award, it became big news anyway, with reporters and cameras waiting at her door to catch her when she left the house. "I didn't want to make a big thing out of it, but I needed to stay true to my values, and I could not share this award because with winning five medals, it just didn't make sense.

"I could not accept a shared award, because what does it say about the sport? What does it say to other kids with disabilities if, after winning five medals and setting world records, I can't win Athlete of the Year but have to share with someone who did not even finish their race, although she had a great season?

"That was my main reason. I felt sorry for Perdita because she didn't ask for that. I didn't want to do it against her, that's for sure. I had no pleasure in doing it, but I had to speak out. I don't regret it, and I think, yes, it was courageous at the time and hard. How much impact does it have? Well, I don't know.[4]

"Now they've separated the prizes — they've got Para Athlete of the Year and Athlete of the Year, which, in my view, is not better."

Chantal believes that Paralympians can and should be viewed as competing at the same level as Olympians. She argues that if different Olympic sports can be compared, so should Olympic and Paralympic sports. "If we can compare, say, a skater and a kayaker, then we can compare a wheelchair racer and a skater." She says Athletics Canada is "taking the easy way out" by having different awards for para athletes and athletes.

It's also important to Chantal that *any* sport have a depth of field in international competition — both in number of competitors and countries competing. "I've been very judgmental of the Paralympic Movement when sometimes there are not even eight competitors in a final — that's not good for the sport," she says. "Whether it's competitive or not is important, and everybody — starting with the Paralympic Movement — needs to recognize that. Sometimes the Paralympic Movement wants to be fair to everybody, but sport is not fair. Sometimes they lose track of the fact that athletes want highly competitive opportunities."

• • •

In 2016, Chantal was appointed to the Senate of Canada by Prime Minister Trudeau, a role she continues to hold. In a CBC interview after her appointment, she said the biggest question she had before accepting the post was "Is this a place where I can have a real and concrete impact for all Canadians, and the answer was yes."[5]

She says if she had free rein on how to improve the lives of people with disability, her top priority would be "to improve physical access — there should be no excuses." Next, she would focus on access to care and access to services. "I'm thinking about that because of stories we've seen during this pandemic in terms of lack of care, lack of services, and some persons with disability being put in situations of vulnerability because of that."

After that, she says she would reduce the gap in professional opportunities for people with disabilities.

"There is value in investing in education, care, and access, because the more a person has opportunities, the more they will be able to play the part that they want to play in society," she says. "If someone wants to achieve something, they have everything that they need to achieve it."

Chantal has advice for parents of children with disabilities, too. "Don't be overprotective, although it's kind of a human reflex and natural. We want to avoid them being in pain, being at risk, or even being in situations that are uneasy because they're different.

"I remember having a discussion with parents of a boy who was paraplegic, the same as me. Everything being relative, it's quite a light disability involving the legs and a wheelchair, but it involves no learning or speaking impairment. But that kid preferred to be in a specialized school because he was the best there, because he had the least disability. I argued that this is the wrong approach, asking, 'what's going to happen to him at seventeen when he goes to regular life?'

"I understood the parents, and I even understood the kid because it's easier to be the most functional in the school than to be the one who is challenged, and maybe different.

"I mean it's tough; of course it's tougher to have a disability. It takes years to get used to. You go on dates in a wheelchair, and your date is asking questions. As a person with the disability, you will be more often than others out of your comfort zone.

"But if you cocoon yourself or your kids from that, I don't see anything good coming from it, and so my advice is let's try to support them, but make sure that they get into the world with their difference and that they make their space and take their place, the best that they can, with your support. I don't think avoiding being exposed to those challenges is a good approach for the long term."

Chantal adds that it's about "de-dramatizing" as well — not making the disability any worse than it is. "For sure it is a life of challenge, but to dramatize it is not helping anybody. It's not helping the person. It's not helping society."

That approach means not tiptoeing around disability, too. "When kids approach me with questions, I can sometimes feel the stress from their parents, who are thinking, 'I can't believe my kid is asking that.' Or even worse, they say to their child, 'We don't say that, we don't ask that.'" She believes things are improving though: "I think the majority of parents will now let their child be curious and ask valid questions, and let them have that conversation, and I think it is very healthy instead of telling a kid 'don't do that, don't ask that.'"

It works both ways, Chantal says, and people with disability also may need to de-dramatize — by asking for help. "I remember being very fussy that I could do everything myself. And now, sometimes I'll be in a store with a big bag, and someone will be there, and I'll just say, 'Hey, can you hold the door for me?' I didn't do that when I was twenty because I was on a mission to make sure that I could prove to everybody that I could do every single thing, and now I'm more like, 'Let's express what we need and don't need.'

"I think there's some work to do for everyone: to have healthy relationships with people with disabilities, and for people with disabilities to feel good within their own skin," she says.

• • •

Chantal is married to music composer James Duhamel and they have one son, aged seven. The family now lives in Ottawa, Ontario.

She is a proud Canadian, and to mark Canada's 150th anniversary in 2017, she, among others, accepted an invitation to write a "love letter to Canada." In that letter she wrote, "Diversity is not just our signature, it is our strength, and we must never forget it."[6]

Chantal Petitclerc has also never forgotten the small town of Saint-Marc-des-Carrières, in Quebec. A town that nurtured her as she tried to navigate a new reality in her teenage years. A town whose nurturing she has greatly repaid by giving it so much to be proud of.

JERRON HERMAN

What can I contribute to society, to creativity? I contribute all of me.

Jerron is both a professional dancer and writer. He has hemiplegia.

THE ARABESQUE IS A DANCE POSTURE in which the dancer stands on one leg, extends the other leg backward parallel to the ground, bends the torso forward, and extends the arms, one forward and one backward. For any dancer, the arabesque challenges flexibility, balance, and control.

Jerron Herman is a professional dancer and performs a beautiful arabesque. He was born with hemiplegia, a form of cerebral palsy that affects the left side of his body — it causes problems with posture and movement in his left arm and leg.

"I've been told my arabesque is crazy . . . it comes from my left leg shooting up to the air. And my balance is based on my right side being the main impetus for my control, so that these things that were perceived as negatives are now folded into the choreography."[1]

That's how Jerron approaches his dance — turning so-called negatives into art. "I've always been an advocate for people to pursue the antithesis of the thing that is their limitation. Why dance? Primarily because of the physical diagnosis I was given. My body is the instrument, and if I'm a disabled person and my body's the instrument, it's pretty audacious."[1]

For his performance in the world premiere of *Triptych* in 2015, *The New York Times* described him as "the inexhaustible Mr. Herman."[2]

Jerron Herman is both a professional dancer and a professional writer — an interdisciplinary artist.

• • •

Born in 1991, Jerron grew up in Alameda, California, a city across the bay from San Francisco and south of Oakland. He has one older brother, six years his senior.

"I was born under the auspices of the ADA [Americans with Disabilities Act]. Unknown to me, this geographical location — Oakland and Berkeley — was the hotbed of disability justice and the disability rights movements. I was getting a lot of my confidence and understanding of how I could operate in the world through osmosis.

"My brother was a preemie, so my parents already had a very traumatic experience with his birth and hospitalization for six or eight weeks."

Then along came Jerron. He was born full term, but his mom had early suspicions about her second-born, recognizing the problem before even visiting doctors. "She saw that my left hand was closed and wasn't responding to different stimuli. When I was about three months old, she took me to the doctors — they diagnosed hemiplegia . . . They said that I wouldn't be able to clothe myself or feed myself, that I would need assistance for pretty much everything I did."[1]

His parents' acceptance of Jerron's diagnosis was very practical, efficient, and holistic; it was part of their Christian faith. They instilled a deep belief in Jerron that he was whole and didn't have anything lacking. That outlook helped him growing up.

Jerron says, "In my youth, I was a firebrand, always ready to tell someone that I could do something, and always ready to prove myself. It is still a big part of my life to just open up the scope of imagination for folks into what's possible for anyone with a different physicality. It's just like the limits need to be taken off."

In recalling the early treatment of his condition, he says, "I had a very personal vendetta against my diagnosis, against its medicalization, against my schedule of physical therapy/occupational therapy. I had physical therapy three times a week. That meant that I couldn't do different kinds of activities after school. I was just ensconced in medicalization." He adds, "My parents resisted surgeries. I've had no surgeries, and that's unusual."

From the start, art helped him with his diagnosis: "A lot of my upbringing was about how to create space away from my diagnosis, and that's where art came in. My brother is an actor and my parents are closeted artists — they design and they make things. Art was very central to my family and I think that that gave me an initial outlet to "dis" the body. I started to write. Writing and academia were early vehicles for me, where I was able to subvert the physical, to excel, not to be pigeon-holed by my physical prowess."

Growing up as a child in the Bay Area, Jerron had many role models in writers such as Langston Hughes, Claude McKay, Zora Neale Hurston, and Tennessee Williams. He was a big musical theater fan, so Stephen Sondheim and Jonathan Larson also featured. He was a fan of actor Daniel Day Lewis: "When I saw *My Left Foot*, I think that was just a ridiculous moment for me." Classic films were favorites, too. "Cary Grant, Jimmy Stewart, Harry Belafonte, and Paul Newman — I was really intrigued by these solid people," he says.

"I wanted to be a writer since I was in third grade, primarily because I thought it was going to be the only art form that would accept me as a disabled person.[3]

"I was driven by words, by what I would call crafting," he says. "Artistry in art was really my propeller."

• • •

In 2009, Jerron moved to New York City to study dramatic writing at the Tisch School of the Arts, at New York University (NYU). His early ambition was to *not* include disability in his writing, but he later came to embrace it.

He says, "I loved the traditional way of study. I loved studying to be something. I loved the rigor."

His time at NYU lasted only one year because of financial insecurity, however. But after a series of side jobs, he returned to study at The King's College, graduating in 2013 with a bachelor's degree in media, culture, and the arts.

Unlike his long-held ambition to be a writer, his introduction to dance was serendipitous. While studying at King's, he did an internship at the New Victory Theater. Never having danced before, he worked with choreographer Sean Curran, who told him he had good movement.

Sean introduced Jerron to his friend Heidi Latsky, artistic director of her own dance company in New York City. The Heidi Latsky Dance Company integrates dancers with disabilities. Physically integrated dance has become more common in recent years, especially in the UK and United States.

Jerron joined the company in the summer of 2011, somewhat to his own surprise. "I didn't even have the ambition for dance like I had for writing. I was really being led by different people."

He stayed with the company for eight years, until 2019, always as dancer, but also as associate and development director. During this time, Jerron performed at venues such as the Lincoln Center and the Whitney Museum of American Art.

. . .

For Jerron, the elements of professional dancing are wide ranging — from embracing beauty and movement to pursuing a physical art form with a disability, and more.

"The mental process to start dancing was the first thing — having these really established people telling me that I could do this," he says. "I was ready for something that would say 'this is the closed door, let's open it.'[3]

"I always loved to move. It was always a matter of knowing that my movement is naturally beautiful; it was thought of as beautiful; it was going to be in the places we go to see beautiful things. To be in those places as a disabled person really elevated my idea of what vehicle was or what could be consumed as beautiful."[3]

In dance, his hemiplegia remains a challenge: "The disability is still affecting my body — there is no 'because I'm dancing I have less of a disability.' In fact . . . I could do all these great feats sometimes and then sometimes I'll have a spasm in my left arm that will make it more difficult to do my arabesque or to dance across the stage."[3]

Jerron compares physical therapy with dance; he recognizes the similarities of the tasks and movements, the attention to detail, and the intensity, but finds that the end goal in dance makes more sense to him. "In the craziest way, it's the best physical therapy!"[4] In fact, he recently published a commentary on a systematic review of dance and rehabilitation in cerebral palsy in a leading medical journal.[5]

With dance, Jerron has been able to pursue the antithesis of limitation: "There was this glass ceiling that contributed to my pursuits in other art forms [writing] . . . With dance you could use the body that you were told was fractured and incomplete and you were able to use it in a way that spoke volumes, spoke limitlessness, spoke freedom, and spoke facility."[4]

He says, "When I am in the moment, and I'm dancing, I feel this calm . . . Everything is working together, and then some. Dance has relieved me of a stereotype that is placed on people with disabilities."[1]

Jerron also sees dance and writing as overlapping art forms: "I think dance is a new way to write a narrative, and I'm loving this idea that I'm using my body as the story. I'm using my body as the characters and the words that I want to say. I'm actually an underrepresented character, so whereas [before] I wanted to write underrepresented characters, I'm in the forefront now as a performer."[4]

Looking to the future, Jerron says he wants to be dancer "until I'm forty, fifty — no, eighty." He says, "The glory of an art practice and the glory of getting to extend your body and be onstage and be visible is very compelling."

Plus, he feels like he has a secret weapon, what he calls the "triple crown": "I am disabled, Black, and male, which is fortuitous in dance as it's scarce." He knows there is always the risk of injury that can cut short the career of any professional dancer, but he follows an exercise program to enable and support his dancing.

• • •

Four years after graduating from college, Jerron was named an honoree of The King's College Alumni Association. The award citation reads, in part, "Jerron has become a nationally recognized leader in the world of modern dance. With grace, humor, and inexhaustible joy, he challenges notions about how the human form is viewed and about who can participate at the highest levels of fine arts."[6]

Strong praise for a professional dancer who really only started at age twenty.

After leaving the Heidi Latsky Dance Company in 2019, Jerron became an independent professional dancer. He is also part of a collective called Kinetic Light, a disability arts ensemble, based in New York City and the Bay Area.

His work ethic has brought him success. "Work is where I find my worth," he says. "Being productive is important to me." In 2019 alone, he crafted four world premieres, all full-length evening shows. He had planned for 2020 to be a year of rest and restoration and COVID-19 cemented that plan.

Though dance has brought amazing success over the years, writing remains very important for Jerron. It has been so since childhood. "Writing was my first love. It was the first thing that I felt as a child was my own. It was my voice. Dance was a later voice.

"I'm awed by how writing transports me. I was brought into the world of words. I mean, 'hemiplegia, cerebral palsy' is a mouthful. I had to process and to take on a diagnosis in a way that I had to translate it into lay terms for my friends on the playground. I had to become articulate in a way I now feel was unfair, because a child has to be a child and not have the burden of medical vocabulary. Nevertheless, I do think, in some way, having a complex vocabulary to survive, having to constantly explain myself was a benefit. Because of my diagnosis, I already had an understanding of how words work. It was an introduction to complexity, I think."

In the last few years, Jerron has found expression in combining his two artistic passions of words and dance. He choreographed and performed the solo *Many Ways to Raise a Fist*, a contemplation in word and movement on the meaning of the word "activist" in disability and global history. The premiere was at the Whitney Museum of American Art in 2019 to celebrate the 29th Anniversary of the Americans with Disabilities Act.

In other fields, Jerron has featured as a model for both Tommy Hilfiger and Nike.

• • •

What does it mean to Jerron to be Black, male, and have a disability?

"I do think all three of those identities coalesce in lovely ways, and I draw from them, and they help each other in a sense. I think I have more of an immediate or deeper sense of my Blackness than my disability because that was primarily where I was taught — it was church and all the things like that.

"My cultural artifacts were more Black; there's less for disability, so that's why I am trying to create more around disability."

Growing up, he experienced more discrimination because of his disability than his race. "I think that was primarily because of being in the liberal west. There was already an understanding around racism; people were striving to be inclusive. But disability was still so unknown that people were just fumbling around me and around disability. I never attributed my hardships to race, ever. The first time I was called the N-word was at NYU, among my peers.

"Throughout adolescence, there were always people making fun of my gait or my arm." He remembers an incident in school when he had received a number of awards and a jealous classmate mimicked his arm movement. "I realized I had to come to terms with the fact that my productivity, my work ethic — these attributes of my personality — were what might be causing the problem, not so much my disability or race."

As for the world of dating, Jerron says, "that's where disability has been particularly fun to think through, and to articulate, because I think that there's still a desire for men to present a kind of prowess in the physical realm. Though I'm a dancer, and I'm physical, people still wonder — 'Could he pick me up? Could he protect me?' These questions have been posed to me." Jerron believes that there's a kind of a stereotype of Black men being proficient, being protective, and being strong, but that those qualities weren't always allotted to him.

However, Jerron finds freedom from all that in his art: "As an artist I don't have to be beholden to anyone's dictum of what it means to be male, what it means to be Black, and what it means to be disabled. When I became an artist, it kind of shed all of the expectations of each category. I do hold fast to my views of all of those things, but I also don't let them be my shackle. I'm so drawn to art because it is not dictating."

Jerron is busy in both the general arts and culture space, and the disability space. He is very thoughtful about his activism — what aspects of justice he is attached to, and what issues he individually and collectively wants to craft the conversation around. One example is the lack of services for adults with cerebral palsy: "The condition is only dealt with in the first years. The disability remains for life, but not the services. It literally felt like I was kicked out the door when I was sixteen. 'Okay, go fend for yourself.'"

Since 2017, he has served on the board of trustees, and is currently vice-chair, of Dance/USA — the largest organization for dancers in the U.S., and one that emphasizes inclusion and represents dancers of all abilities. He is also involved with the National Dance Institute's DREAM project, a program to bring children with and without disabilities together to dance and perform as an ensemble. He is a 2020 Disability Futures Fellow, a joint initiative of the Andrew W. Mellon and Ford Foundations. He also continues to be an ambassador for the Cerebral Palsy Foundation.

$$\bullet\ \bullet\ \bullet$$

Jerron has this advice about following your passion: "I think that a lot of people are born into limitation; are born into expectations that limit them. If there's something that you really want to do, you should do it. I love for my dancing to represent that we always want opportunities to be excellent, to be beautiful and to be artful."[3]

On his website Jerron questions: "What can I contribute to society, to creativity?" and he answers, "I contribute all of me."[7]

Jerron Herman is definitely inexhaustible.

ELLIE COLE

Better to get a sore neck from aiming too high than a hunchback from aiming too low.

Ellie is an Australian Paralympic swimmer.
She is an amputee as a result of cancer.

CENTERED ON THE PROMOTIONAL POSTER for the documentary film *Rising Phoenix*, Ellie Cole floats in a sea of stillness, with a spotlight highlighting both her body and the blueness of the water surrounding her. Ellie's arms are outstretched, with a slight bend in her elbows and wrists. Her legs exhibit grace and contrast: her left leg outstretched with toes pointing downwards, while her right leg, amputated above the knee, reflects a glimmer of light.

The illumination of Ellie's figure on the poster evokes a dual sense of optimism and determinism, two core components of Ellie's spirit. With her participation in the film, released on Netflix in 2020, she hopes to showcase the multidimensional nature of the Paralympic Movement.

"It's the strangest thing, but I always forget I have one leg. When I see photos like that, I'm like 'boom, there it is.' It looks so cool," Ellie has said.[1]

Ellie was born in 1991 in a suburb of Melbourne, Australia, healthy and strong. It wasn't until she turned two that she began to get sick. Her mom found a bump behind her right knee, and that bump turned out to be a very rare form of cancer — a neurosarcoma. After many rounds of chemotherapy that made Ellie even sicker and the tumor no smaller, her parents opted to have her leg amputated. All this before Ellie turned three years old.

In a childhood video filmed after her surgery, Ellie can be heard saying, "I want my foot back," as she sits in a wheelchair eyeing her new prosthetic leg. Her mom's voice is in the background, encouraging her, "This *is* your foot, isn't it Ellie? It's staying right where it is."[2]

For Ellie's parents, that was a heartbreaking time. There was an element of trauma surrounding Ellie's surgery. They witnessed, however, their young daughter's endless energy and her zest for living life to the fullest, and they didn't want her to face any limitations.

As Ellie recovered from surgery and adapted to life as an amputee, she was never told "this is too much" or "don't overdo it." Her eagerness to experience life trumped any professional medical opinion that her parents received, and so they adopted an attitude of acceptance, letting her go out in the world to see what she could do.

"In a way, they felt pretty torn. On one hand, my disability was a whole new world for them. Whatever they were told, they were going to believe," says Ellie. "On the other hand, they had this three-year-old girl who wanted to get out there and just tear into everything and experience and achieve as much as possible, every single day. They didn't want to hold me back, which I'm very grateful for."

Her mom allowed her a high degree of freedom and trusted her, just as she did Ellie's siblings. Both her parents made sure not to pile on limitations or keep her in Bubble Wrap.

"When I reflect on my childhood, I was pretty adventurous," says Ellie. "My twin sister and I were quite imaginative, as most kids are. We played pirates, and cops and robbers. We even set up a permanent campsite in the forest nearby, stocked with books and games and whistles. When I think back, I was just always outside, full of adventure. We were never inside, except to eat and sleep."

When it came time to enter school, Ellie was ready to pave her own independent path — one that led her to the swimming pool.

• • •

South of Melbourne, on the outskirts of the city, Ellie's primary school sits nestled between a playground and nature reserve. Only three miles away, the fresh sea air of Port Phillip Bay gusts along the Australian coast. Inside the school, ten-year-old Ellie is the only student with a disability. Sporting her red-and-blue uniform, she walks with friends into the school gym and picks up a basketball. As she shoots, she sees her PE teacher, Ms. Harris, approach.

"Ellie, I saw the Paralympics on TV, showing athletes with disabilities," says Ms. Harris. "I know you really enjoy competing at the swimming carnivals every year. This is a great way for you to represent our school at Nationals."

By that age, Ellie had already tried a number of sports and had landed on swimming. It was one of the few sports that allowed her to forget her disability. Doctors originally recommended that Ellie take up swimming to regain strength, thinking it would take her a year just to learn how to swim in a straight line. Instead, it took Ellie just two weeks — and her swift progression continued from there.

She has said of that time, "One of my favorite things to do [was to] beat people with two legs. So I did that a lot as a kid and I think that's what made me such a successful athlete now."[3]

Once her teacher told her about Para sports, Ellie's parents encouraged her to get involved. They took her to her first wheelchair sports event, a Junior Nationals nearby in Adelaide. She met all sorts of athletes, and everyone had a physical disability.

"My mind was blown," says Ellie. "I never knew that there were other people like me. I remember everyone was comparing their disabilities and showing everybody what was wrong with them. It was kind of like 'the more different you are, the more cool you are.' In the outside world it wasn't like that at all. I met athletes there that I'm still friends with to this day."

Ellie discovered a newfound pride in being an amputee. She discovered that when she surrounded herself with similar people, they accepted her straightaway and gave her the confidence to be herself. That early experience — finding a community in youth sports — is something that Ellie sees immense value in.

"I'm a big believer in grassroots sports and in developing young athletes," says Ellie. "I want to get into that area once I'm finished with elite swimming. There's so much potential in young kids who haven't learned yet about discrimination or limitations. They haven't been told 'you can't do X, Y, or Z.' I just want to get in there as soon as I can and unleash that a bit more."

That early conversation with her PE teacher had a butterfly effect.[4] "It was just a little conversation on the basketball courts at my primary school that just led to everything else," says Ellie. She had no idea it would open up a whole career, allowing her to travel and compete on the world stage.

· · ·

In the Cole household, Ellie's mom would take the time to sit down with each of her four kids, one at a time, encouraging them to reflect — to talk about their feelings — and then asking what they thought their potential could be. Ellie enjoyed goal setting, and as a young girl she would write down those goals and stick them on the wall. Seeing them every day kept her on track.

"I always had big goals when I was younger. I had a lot of people not expecting too much of me, and so I expected a lot from myself, to prove them wrong," says Ellie. "A lot of people don't sit down and reflect on what they're able to do, or what they can potentially do. They just go with the flow. But for me, I was always goal setting."

What were those goals?

Thinking of her favorite quote, "better to get a sore neck from aiming too high than a hunchback from aiming too low," she says, "I wanted to be the fastest athlete that has ever walked the planet."

That drive to be the best — which included training alongside nondisabled Olympic power athletes — took her on an impressive path: she is a six-time Paralympic gold medalist, winning a total of fifteen medals to date across three Paralympic Games. She is one of Australia's most successful athletes, holding a host of national and world records.

When she was in seventh grade, Ellie completed a questionnaire about where she would be when she graduated from high school. She wrote that she would be beating her idol, Canadian swimmer Stephanie Dixon. After graduation, Ellie had the chance to open that questionnaire and proudly reflect that she had done just that: beaten Stephanie the year prior in Beijing 2008, Ellie's first trip to the Paralympics.

Another competitor Ellie looked up to was Natalie du Toit, the South African Paralympic swimmer.

"I remember the first time I laid eyes on her," says Ellie. "She was swimming up and down the pool, and I was so excited; she's the queen to me. She smashed me for years. I didn't beat her until London 2012, at her last swimming competition. That was my life goal: I knew I could die happy if I did that. But once I did beat her, I felt this overwhelming sense of guilt that I had dethroned my hero. I felt terrible. It was a really interesting reaction."

After London 2012, Ellie underwent a series of major shoulder reconstruction surgeries. Determined to bounce back, she endured twelve months of rehabilitation. She also began competing in the national wheelchair basketball league, earning the league's award for Best New Talent in her first season. Rehab could be lonely, and participating in a team sport relieved some of that.

But swimming ultimately lured her back. Ellie gained immense confidence at the 2015 World Championships, where she broke multiple world records and took home five medals. The following year, at the Rio 2016 Paralympic Games, she won six medals, earning a spot on the podium for each of the events she competed in.

"I've won quite a number of Paralympic medals, but when I reflect on my swimming career, I think of all the times I've been through that have been extremely difficult, like my shoulder reconstructions," says Ellie. "There were times I wanted to give up, but in those moments, I just kept going. Those are the times I'm really proud of — the struggles and getting through those.

"Over the last fifteen years, what is important to me has completely changed. When I was twelve, all I wanted to do was win gold medals, and I've since realized that's not entirely what it's all about. I've been so proud to compete in the Games. It definitely hasn't been easy, but it's been a lot of fun."

•••

Today, Ellie is an Australian icon.

As she reflects on all that she has achieved, she says that what she values most are the doors that life has opened to her. She sees her disability as an asset, not a burden. She has publicly said, "Life's a precious gift. I don't want to waste that. If you offered me the chance to go back twenty years and have two legs, I would say no."[5]

Ellie is a strong advocate for others with disability. She is an ambassador for Ability First Australia and has been recognized with a series of awards: Vogue Game Changer, *Cosmopolitan Magazine*'s Sportswoman of the Year, and Westpac 100 Women of Influence. In 2019, she earned a bachelor's degree in health and exercise science from Australian Catholic University. And on top of all of that, she has received the Medal of Order of Australia, an honor recognizing Australian citizens for their outstanding achievements.

Across every platform, Ellie spreads her message, reframing what's possible with a physical disability. Her personal mission is to "reinvent the wheel on how people perceive others with a disability."[6]

And her message seems to be sticking. She says, "I've noticed that I've been getting treated differently around the pool deck. People don't talk about me in a condescending way anymore. When they talk to me, it's as if I'm more of a role model, rather than somebody who's here and just giving it their best shot. And so I have definitely seen a change in that."

•••

Training in 2020 in the times of COVID-19 presented a whole new set of challenges, but because of her experience in sport, Ellie was able to adapt to new environments. She had to learn how to change her training regimen while pools were closed and find ways to stay in top form when travel to competitions was limited. As a result, she's developed a resilience that she knows will pay off for decades to come.

As she contemplates her next major competition, the postponed Paralympic Games in Japan, she says, "It's going to be a new evolved style of athlete in Tokyo. Because of COVID-19 restrictions on athlete training and competitions, athletes will have to fight so hard to be there, so it's going to be an extra dimension that we've never seen in an athlete."

• • •

Ellie's determination to prepare for top performance at the next Paralympics is helped by technology, too. Today she uses the Ottobock Genium X3, a waterproof, robotic prosthesis that helps her train and provides more mobility. It was designed in partnership with the U.S. Army, who dedicates funding for prosthetics research to support veterans.

Ellie is thrilled to have the opportunity to use such technology, but she is well aware that many of those advancements are out of reach for the vast majority of amputees, because of price. She hopes to change that.

"Toyota funded the leg for me and it's been a complete game changer," says Ellie. "I can walk down hills now without worrying about falling over, and I can walk in the ocean or go surfing. To think they are only going to get better is comforting for me. I would like to see prosthetics become more widely available for people who don't have $150,000 to spend. It's a shame that the only people who can walk on these legs are from the army or from rich families. When it comes to disability, everybody should have equal opportunity."

• • •

When Ellie was approached about participating in the film *Rising Phoenix*, a documentary telling the stories of nine Paralympic athletes, she jumped at the chance to help, to give back to the Paralympic Movement that has given so much to her. She had no idea how much attention she'd get as a result.

"Six months after production finished, I found out that the film would be on Netflix in 180 countries," says Ellie. "I couldn't believe it. Once it aired, I got hundreds and hundreds of emails, most of them in Spanish. People didn't really understand what the Paralympics are, and they were even more outraged that we went through so many issues in terms of funding. I thought, 'Wow, this is going to change the world.' And it pretty much did, so I'm very happy."

When the film was released, in spring 2020 in the midst of the pandemic, Ellie watched it for the first time at home alone, like everyone else around the world. Both her parents and sister had given the production team footage, some of which Ellie had never seen before — like her mom's reaction watching Ellie win her first Paralympic medal.

"I was watching that scene with the rest of the world, which was really strange. [In the film] I saw Mom go from being really upset about me losing my leg to all of a sudden fast forward fifteen years showing how proud she was of me."

She hopes everyone can see the film — to hear and see the impact of the Paralympic Movement, one that she knows can inspire all.

That's her message in the film: "I want as many people in the world to see the Paralympics as possible, because if my parents had known about the Paralympics back when I was three years old, they would have had so much more hope in what people with disabilities can do."[2]

JIM ABBOTT

More has been given to you than was ever taken away

Jim is a professional speaker and former Major League Baseball pitcher. He was born without a right hand.

Saturday, September 4, 1993, Yankee Stadium

The damp afternoon game on the Labor Day weekend has drawn a relatively small crowd. At the top of the ninth, the Yankees are up 4–0, and a win seems a sure thing. But it's not the score that makes this day memorable.

The Yankee pitcher faces the batter with two men already out. The batter hits a grounder to the shortstop, who easily picks it up and fires the ball to first base.

Game over.

The crowd roars, not so much for the win as for the pitcher, who is being mobbed on the field by his teammates for accomplishing what few others have ever done — pitching a no-hitter in Yankee Stadium.

Almost twenty years later, that pitcher recalled the day: "I'd been practicing that last pitch, that last out [since I was a kid] . . . It took a long time to leave the field, in part because I didn't want to. I didn't want anyone picking up the trash just yet, or hosing this moment away."[1]

Tony Kubik, who was in the booth that day calling the game for television, described it as "one of the most wonderful moments . . . for as sweet a man as there is in any uniform in a major sport."[2]

That "sweet man" was Jim Abbott, who just entered the Major League Baseball (MLB) record books — and who happened to have been born without a right hand.

• • •

Jim was born in Flint, Michigan, in 1967 to eighteen-year-old parents Mike and Kathy. Two weeks later his parents married in the morning, and then went to their respective new roles in the afternoon — Kathy caring for their baby, and Mike working his new job at the General Motors plant.

Had academically gifted Kathy not been a young mom, she might have completed her teaching degree — she was just two semesters short. Had gifted athlete Mike not been a young dad, he might have gone to college — instead he went straight from last semester at high school to a factory job.

Mike worked to pay the bills and Kathy stayed home to raise Jim, and then Chad, who followed four years later. When Jim was in middle school, his mom returned to her studies to complete a law degree.

Jim says, "My parents were really growing up together. They made tremendous sacrifices, but they had tremendous resilience and strength that I think they attained through the trials they went through. Times were definitely difficult. They stuck together, even though I think at times that was difficult, as well. I have to pay homage to them. My brother and I take tremendous pride in how they made it through."

Having been born with only one hand, Jim fought insecurity as a young boy. Whenever he had the chance, he would go outside alone, with just his ball and glove. In his memoir, *Imperfect: An Improbable Life*, he has written of those early days:

There, out of sight, away from the world, I was free to dream. With no one staring or judging, I'd stand in front of the brick wall, a rubber-coated ball in my left hand, my Dusty Baker glove hooded over my right wrist, and I'd throw, and catch, and chase, and switch the glove back and forth. The yard was quiet except for the thump against the wall and my footfalls and thick breaths that followed, all in pursuit of the baseball . . . Inside the house, Mom was . . . working through her studies to the tune of the *thump-thump-thump* from behind the far wall.[3]

• • •

Flint, Michigan, where Jim grew up, is known as "Vehicle City" and home to General Motors. It's had its share of infamy over the years for its financial crises, high crime rate, and public health emergencies. The strength of Flint, however, was its people: supportive parents, friends, teachers, and coaches who recognized its problems and sought to offer alternatives for the city's kids — opening gyms at night for the kids to play volleyball and basketball, for example, to keep them off the streets. This resulted in a lot of great athletes coming from this tough city.

One of those great people in Jim's life was his third-grade teacher, Mr. Clarkson, who walked with a limp and knew what it felt like to be "different." And while the two rarely talked about their "shared bond," it was acknowledged in acts of kindness. One day while the rest of the class was watching a film, Mr. Clarkson took two chairs outside to the hallway, and patiently taught Jim how to tie his shoelaces with one hand.

Jim also benefited from some early great coaches who took the time to figure out small adjustments so that he could play successfully. That support was enough to allow Jim to play both football and baseball in high school — and to excel in both. But his passion was baseball, and his skill as a pitcher soon brought him to the attention of college coaches and professional scouts.

. . .

In 1985, Jim entered the University of Michigan, roughly an hour's drive from Flint. There he played baseball for the college, winning two Big Ten championships and making the U.S. baseball team, the latter a pivotal time in his life.

"Playing for the U.S. team was an integral part of my growth as a person and as a baseball player," he says. "We met up at a training camp in a small town in Tennessee. At that time, the U.S. baseball team was all amateur players, all college kids. And so, you found yourself on the field with all these guys that you've heard about. I was from northern Michigan — everyone teased me, asking, 'Do they even play baseball up there?'

"To make that team and compete with those guys and play for the U.S. — it was amazing. Playing for the U.S. was the best team experience I ever had. It wasn't glamorous; we traveled to minor league ballparks around the country, ate at a lot of community potlucks, drove on school buses, stayed at cheap motels.

"We went to Cuba, Japan, and Italy. Coming together for the purpose of getting to the Olympics and maybe winning the gold medal was just a beautiful experience."

"The team" was always paramount to Jim: "From high school right through to the MLB, my teammates were incredible. I always felt so welcomed and embraced by my teammates. The locker room was my place of refuge. It was my sense of belonging.

"Playing for the U.S. team gave me the belief that if I'm playing with, say, this guy who's going to have a major league career, maybe I can too."

In 1987, Jim was the flag-bearer for Team USA at the Pan American Games in Indianapolis, where the team came in second place. That same year, he won the James E. Sullivan Award as the top amateur athlete in the United States — the only baseball player to do so to date.

In 1988, Jim won a silver medal with the national team at the Baseball World Cup in Rome, and followed that soon after with the highlight of his amateur career — winning a gold medal with the team at the Seoul Olympic Games, where baseball was a demonstration sport.

Many years later, Jim would be honored by being elected to the College Baseball Hall of Fame (2007) and by the University of Michigan retiring his number 31 jersey (2009).

• • •

After his success at the Olympics, Jim began his MLB professional career in 1989. Over the next decade, he played for the California Angels, New York Yankees, Chicago White Sox, and Milwaukee Brewers. These were rewarding — but challenging — years.

"Although I was talented, in order for me to compete and be successful, I had to work incredibly hard, to stay right on the knife's edge of what I could do." He says, "It was highly competitive."

A tough part of playing at the professional level is being traded, Jim says, and having to leave your team and teammates at a moment's notice. "You can be just completely unmoored and traded to a different side of the country and expected to perform and then traded again, and released. It's a gauntlet.

"It's wonderful and incredibly rewarding. I would go back there in a second, if I could, but it is definitely difficult."

Jim briefly retired after the 1996 season, returned in 1998, and finally hung up his glove after the 1999 season.

• • •

When asked what his career high was, Jim names two — the final at the Olympics in Seoul and the no-hitter in Yankee Stadium.

"I can't separate the two. I love them equally, but for different reasons. What I'm most proud about with both of those accomplishments is that I was out there for the ninth inning — the last out — of both games. The excitement and tension and hopefulness in both still give me a big smile and goosebumps.

"To want something that badly. To have to manage those emotions. The anxiety. And to go back to the process and perform, to make it through, and to get to that last out, is just an indescribable feeling. I wanted it at the beginning of the ninth inning in both games. I don't know that you could want something to happen more. To have it work out.

"I just can't say that one was better than the other. I love the team aspect of the Olympics. I love the guys on that team, and we celebrated as a team. I don't know that any of us will ever have that kind of experience again. The no-hitter, of course, is a team experience, because you have a lot of help. But it is personal in some ways too; it sort of lends validation. It's one game, and it takes a lot of luck."

• • •

Being famous for being a *one-handed* player was, as Jim describes, "an internal battle."

It takes a lot of extra practice to throw and catch with one hand. Over the years, he mastered a complex glove exchange from one hand to the other, after "a million tries and nearly as many clumsy failures"[4] — and did it consistently at speed, without dropping ball or glove.

His innate talent, persistence, and solution-driven approach were qualities that Jim developed in spades from a young age. His ability soon drew attention from the press.

"I started to do pretty well when I was twelve years old, and attention came along with that. The local newspaper wrote an article about me, and there was a picture of me. At each step when I did well, there was more attention. Then there were these awards but they were always a 'courage award,' or the 'most determined award,' or the 'most inspirational award.'

"To be honest, that wore thin. I tired of that. I wanted to be known as a good player.

"I have a hard time saying this, but I greatly admire just getting in the game and participating, and I encourage that. But for me, I didn't want to just participate. I wanted to be good. And I felt like I had enough talent to be good. And if I worked hard enough, I could be good.

"I pushed back a little bit, at some points, at some of the attention that came my way strictly because of my hand.

"When the U.S. team traveled to places like Japan and Cuba, a big deal was made of my hand. The story seemed to precede us, and it was really a big part of the attention our team received. My teammates teased me a little bit, but they never resented that, or made fun of it. In fact, they sort of circled around me and made me feel protected and sort of helped to shield me from some of the attention when it did get a little bit overwhelming."

When Jim made it to the MLB, in the early days, in every town he traveled to there was a television camera and a local newspaper columnist with a flowery story to write. He struggled with that — knowing the attention was for his disability rather than his capability as an athlete.

That struggle eased somewhat when he came to realize he could use the attention to help others. "In every town we went to, there were families that came to the ballpark, with kids missing a hand, or part of an arm. As we met with those families, I started to understand the impact that someone like me playing in the major leagues could have for those families, for those kids. I wanted the message to be more than just participation. I felt it could be as impactful or even more saying, 'Yes, you can play, but you can also succeed. You can do things differently and still do them just as well as other people, or maybe even better.'

"So that became part of my message.

"And that fame has been a push and pull my whole life. I do feel more at ease with all of that now than I ever did before, but I had to go through that feeling of 'let me be who I think I can be as a pitcher — *how well* I can pitch, rather than *how* I pitch.' That was always a tension in my baseball playing career, especially in the first four or five years of my major league career."

・・・

Jim wrote his memoir, with Tim Brown, in 2012. The title, *Imperfect: An Improbable Life*, was the suggestion of his editor, and Jim thought it was exactly right.

"I thought it was a great title. Some people disagreed — they didn't like the idea that someone with a physical disability would be considered imperfect. I feel they missed the point — the point is coming to appreciate imperfection; coming to appreciate the blessings that come from the obstacles and challenges along the way.

"The running metaphor was the imperfection of that 1993 no-hitter game — although it was a great milestone and a great achievement, it was by no means perfect.

"Telling my story has been a journey of understanding who I am and the journey that I've been on, which is a lot of coming to terms with being born missing a right hand. I was very lucky and had a lot of blessings, but I definitely struggled with the insecurity of being different. I definitely struggled with how it felt to be on the outside looking in, how it felt to have to learn to do things differently every step of the way.

"My baseball career was so rewarding in so many ways — in the places I had a chance to play, the people I met, the experiences I had. But in some ways it was a reckoning as well. I used sports — sports were a tremendous way of hiding from all those feelings that I had, all that insecurity. Let's imagine that insecurity as being a sort of void. It was easy to fill it with sports — winning, success, newspaper articles, television, scholarships, the U.S. team and Olympic team. That's tremendously great and it does give you a sense of self-worth.

"Until you lose."

He says, "It was when I ran up against failure at the professional level that I had to come to terms with some things that baseball hadn't quite filled. In writing the book, I really had to look into those feelings that bubble below the surface, feelings that I didn't always know were there. You just keep moving along until all of a sudden, you have to deal with them. I did that in a very public way under the scrutiny of MLB, the media, and fans.

"It's been an interesting journey. In order for me to go out into the real world post-baseball, I had to really come to terms with a lot of feelings that I had, and how I had been dealing with them up until that point."

• • •

Jim cares a lot about the many families and children with disability who reached out to him throughout his career and who still continue to contact him to this day.

"I still get cards and letters, emails, and tweets from parents with kids who have similar disabilities and challenges as I do, from the U.S. and from around world. In my office I have a desk full of stationery, pictures, and cards. I find myself replying a lot to try to answer that need in a very specific, niche way. My book is an attempt to answer those questions in long form that I can't always really sum up in a one-paragraph letter.

"When I get a letter from a parent or family member talking about a child, the only ones that I worry about are the ones who are incredibly protective of their kids, who shield them from experience, and who want to say, 'You're perfect just the way you are.'

"I understand that message, but everything that I try to convey is, 'Yes, I know that it's tough, I remember that. I remember middle school. I remember hiding my hand in my pocket. I remember feeling very insecure, and feeling very much on the outside looking in, and I have a feeling that you're probably going to go through that too, but that's okay to feel that way.'

"As you get older, those times don't happen as often, they don't last as long.

"Having gone through those times, you seem to find the strength to deal with those experiences because they're always there — they're lifelong — but you seem to build up the strength to deal with them in a much better, more balanced way.

"I do believe that honesty is very important. It's not easy. We're not perfect. We won't feel up to every challenge. It's okay when challenges come along, to feel pushed to the brink. We'll get through those challenges. We will do it.

"But remember, you have it within you to hang in there, to beat it. You might just barely get by, but you're going to win. You're going to be stronger the next time it comes around.

"That's a lot to say to a twelve-year-old, or the parents of a child with disability.

"I guess that's my message in a nutshell."

...

A different sort of challenge faced Jim after retiring from professional baseball — the same challenge many athletes experience.

"Retirement is a painful transition. The part that has bolstered your self-esteem and who you felt you were — when you don't have that anymore, it's really tough. You feel emptiness."

What has helped to sustain him through both those tough professional years and now in his retirement is his marriage in 1991 to Dana and the birth of his two daughters, Maddy and Ella.

Still, he says, "It's hard to find purpose, 'What do I do now? Where do I find that fulfillment?' You have to find something to direct that energy and that passion toward.

"Then I feel guilt because I really was so blessed. I did very well financially in the game and I have a beautiful wife and two daughters."

Today, Jim enjoys a successful speaking career. (Currently, the COVID-19 pandemic has curtailed his speaking engagements, though some has moved online.) "I was lucky," he says. "That gave me an outlet."

• • •

It's now almost three decades since that Labor Day weekend in Yankee Stadium. Thinking back on his life that afternoon in the ballpark and beyond, Jim remembers those early days in Flint and two young parents repeating to their child, "More has been given to you than was ever taken away."

Words to live by.

TOM SHAKESPEARE

Different, but in a good way

Tom is a social scientist, bioethicist, and
academic. He has restricted growth.

ON HIS WEBSITE, Tom Shakespeare describes his foray into online dating:

Finding myself unaccountably single, and dissatisfied with that state of affairs . . . I decided to do what all middle-aged middle-class people do, and advertise. The [dating] website was quite particular. Lots of questions about interests and desires. I was about to put myself out there when a question arose. What to say about disability? Would it be a turn-off to admit that not only did I have dwarfism, but that I am also now in a wheelchair? Could a date with a cripple possibly appear attractive? I could withhold the truth, only to disappoint later. Or I could come clean, and risk no responses at all. In the end, I was frankly coy. My slogan was 'different, but in a good way,' and from my photographs it was clear that I had a disability.[1]

Dwarfism is also known as "achondroplasia" and "restricted growth" — the latter is Tom's preferred term for the condition. Just over a decade ago, in his early forties, Tom became paralyzed and now mostly uses a wheelchair for mobility.

A social scientist and bioethicist, Tom is an academic who writes, talks, and researches mainly about disability, but also about ethical issues. He graduated with a bachelor's degree from Cambridge University, later returning to complete a master's and PhD. Over his working life, he has held positions as lecturer and research fellow at UK universities. He also worked at the World Health Organization in Geneva, where one of his contributions was helping to produce the *World Report on Disability*. His current position is Professor of Disability Research at the London School of Hygiene and Tropical Medicine. He has published approximately one hundred papers and chapters, and authored or edited fourteen books. He regularly talks to academic, professional, and lay audiences around the world and broadcasts on BBC Radio 4. Tom's website, cleverly titled Farmer of Thoughts, is a wonderful compendium of his work.[2] The abundant crop of thoughts this farmer produces is sufficient to feed many people interested in disability issues.

And if all that wasn't enough, Tom has also performed as a stand-up comedian and in one-man shows, and has emceed in the disability arts world. He has taken part in contemporary dance performances, created artwork, and written about contemporary visual art. He has served on the Arts Council of England and chaired Arts Council England, North East.

Tom's formal title is Sir Thomas William Shakespeare, 3rd Baronet, FBA. The baronet title is inherited from his grandfather, one Tom is embarrassed by and chooses not to use.[3] But he is proud of the FBA, which denotes his election as a Fellow of the British Academy. And by the way, as for the oft-asked question of being related to that "other Shakespeare" — the famous poet and playwright — Tom says, "If all . . . ifs and buts and suppositions were right . . . Shakespeare's grandfather Thomas would be my direct ancestor, and he and I would be . . . well, cousins, albeit very many times removed."[4]

Tom grew up in England; his father was a doctor, his mother a nurse. He has a younger brother and an older half brother. He has two children and one grandchild. Restricted growth runs in the family. His dad, Tom himself, and Tom's two adult children all have it. But for Tom's grandfather, having a child with restricted growth came as a surprise: "When my father was born in 1927, my grandfather reacted with horror and shame to a birth [of a child with restricted growth] that was completely unexpected."[5]

Consequently, Tom's grandfather advised his son never to have children, because the chances were too great that they, too, would have restricted growth. But Tom's father chose his own life course, accepting the odds of having a child with restricted growth rather than the alternative of having no children at all.

Tom didn't hear the story of his grandfather's advice until long after the older man's death. It came as a shock to him, as his grandfather had always been very kind to him. But disapproval was an attitude he came up against again when he was about to become a father himself.

For Tom and his then partner, living in a time of "right to choose," their decision to continue with the pregnancy having found out that their child would have restricted growth was a strong, positive statement about quality of life. They made that decision despite pressure from many to terminate the pregnancy — including Tom's mother, who admitted that that would have been her choice, had abortion been available in the UK in the 1960s.

Of the medical advice they received, Tom says, "At the time it was an irritation, but in retrospect, the medical attitude seems shocking to me. None of the clinicians would have known as much about achondroplasia as I did, who'd lived with it for more than twenty years, and whose father had lived with it for fifty years. They had no reservations about making it clear to a couple, one of whom had the condition, that it was advisable not to have a baby with achondroplasia. The experience shaped my views about genetics, and about the medical profession, for many years to come. It made me skeptical of the rhetoric about non-directive counselling and informed consent. I suspected that lurking under the new terminology was the same old fear of having a disabled child."[5]

• • •

Tom's first role model was his father, who taught him important lessons from an early age. Growing up with restricted growth didn't seem odd to Tom since he was "just like Dad." When young Tom noticed people staring at him, his dad would advise him to just ignore it. Throughout his life, Tom has been the object of unwelcome comments and stares, but he learned how to handle them, thanks to his dad.

As a voracious reader, young Tom also found other early role models in fiction. *The Chronicles of Narnia*, by C.S. Lewis, *The Lord of the Rings*, by J.R.R. Tolkien, and later books by authors such as Alan Garner all showed dwarfs were noble people — sturdy, warlike, humorous — not figures of fun. Tom says that as a young boy, he somewhat identified with those characters and found this fantasy world appealing.

Later, when Tom was in his twenties, other people became his role models — people who both advocated for and who lived with disability. They included people like Judy Heumann, Kalle Könkkölä, Mike Oliver, Vic Finkelstein, Jenny Morris, and the recently deceased Sian Vasey. Meeting these people inspired Tom to "come out" as a disabled person and get involved in the political world of disability rights.

On his website, Tom includes short biographies of many other role models — famous and not-so-famous disabled people throughout history — who demonstrate the variety and the achievement of disabled people.

...

Although inspired by many, Tom Shakespeare, "farmer of thoughts," bravely plows his own furrow in both his writing and speaking, highlighting what he considers the important issues of disability. He argues that social barriers are often a more serious problem than the impairments themselves. These barriers include lack of access and negative attitudes.

In his acceptance speech at the University of Sunderland ceremony awarding him an honorary doctorate of science in 2017, in recognition of his outstanding contribution to disability rights, Tom said:

> But disability is all about non-disabled people. You can remove
> barriers. You can challenge stigma and discrimination. You
> can treat people fairly, regardless of their impairment. And in
> all these ways, you can help us build a better world. After
> all, disability will affect your life, one day, even if it hasn't
> yet. You might have a loved one with disability — a parent,
> sibling, partner or child. You might become disabled your-
> self. You almost certainly will experience disability, to be
> fair. Because disability is a fact of life, which affects every
> family in the land. I think this is what the other Shakespeare
> is talking about in *Hamlet*, when he refers to "the thousand
> natural shocks that flesh is heir to."[6]

Tom knows that it is natural for parents to be shocked by the birth of a disabled child, but that disability need not translate into poor quality of life. As his father learned, and as Tom and his own children have learned, "disability need make no difference at all."[5] He says, "Of course, some forms of impairments are more severe than others, and it is understandable that families, and doctors, should wish to avoid lives which are brief, painful or filled with suffering and restriction. But disability is a hugely diverse experience, ranging from trivial differences to serious difficulties . . . Most families quickly come to terms with their disabled child, and most disabled people lead good lives."[5]

Tom supports the right to choose as fiercely as he does disability rights. He wants disabled people to be welcomed in society, but he also wants women and men to have information and choices in pregnancy, and he supports abortion rights. "That means supporting couples to have the test, or to refuse the test, and to have a termination or to continue the pregnancy,"[7] he says.

His concern, though, is the possibility — the danger — of insurers pressuring couples to test or terminate: turning choice into eugenics. He says that parents should not face recriminations for their difficult moral choices, from neither neighbors nor health providers nor insurers. "Choice also requires information: prospective parents need to understand not just about the test, but also about the conditions for which it is offered."[7] He adds that parents need to have balanced information about parenting a child with Down syndrome, for example: the difficulties, but also the joys. He worries that, potentially, fetal DNA tests could identify many different genetic traits, which raises the specter of "tentative pregnancy," and "pick and choose" parenting.[7]

Tom clearly distinguishes between responsibility and guilt. "My grandfather was not old when William [Tom's dad] was born, but the mutation was almost certainly found in his sperm. So he was right to feel responsible, but not right to feel guilty. Modern geneticists counsel patients not to feel shame for something which is beyond their control."[5]

Tom dislikes identity politics. He believes his individualism isn't due to his restricted growth, it's to do with him being Tom Shakespeare. On the one hand, restricted growth *is* him; he looks like he looks and that has shaped his life. But on the other hand, it's not him, because restricted growth is not his sense of self. It's just part of him.

With this attitude, Tom is like most disabled people, wanting to be known for who they are. They want to be loved and respected for themselves, not for being a member of a category. He advocates respecting everybody individually and equally, regardless of disability, race, gender, sexuality, or any other "other." He says, "Sometimes, collective action is a good way to right a wrong, but we need to move through and beyond that into a world in which we can say, 'Look, we're all equals.'

"In the UK, surveys show that negative attitudes [toward disability] are being slowly replaced with more accepting attitudes. This may be to do with higher levels of education and acceptance more generally. It may be to do with greater visibility of disabled achievers in the media — including the effect of televising the Paralympic Games. Familiarity with almost anything makes it less alarming and more accepted." And that includes seeing actors with disabilities in major roles; Tom believes that Peter Dinklage, who has restricted growth and who played the character Tyrion Lannister in *Game of Thrones*, helped make physical disability sexy.

As a dedicated advocate of disability rights, he has some advice for those in positions of power. If he were invited to give advice to the UK prime minister, for example, on how to improve the lives of disabled people, among many suggestions, first would be to train every health worker in disability equality and how to work with disabled people, which would greatly benefit the lives of disabled people and their families. Second would be to decrease the level of poverty among disabled people, which is twice that of nondisabled people. For disabled people who can work, the government should ensure everything possible be done to help and support them to find meaningful employment. And for those who aren't able to work, the government should provide a decent standard of living. His third suggestion would be to provide confidence training for young disabled people.

Tom believes that lack of confidence is one reason why, for example, many disabled people have difficulty with potential partners moving from the "friend" to the "I love you" stage, despite being funny, interesting, lovely, warm people, and having such a lot to give.

He says that disabled people need first to be treated by others as human beings, not as a type. As well, disabled people themselves need to learn to cope with rejection. Everybody gets rejected. Everybody has experience losing to another candidate in a job search. Everybody falls in love with somebody who doesn't want them, and that's painful — nobody can get everybody to fall in love with them or to find them attractive. But disabled people are more likely to have a sense of inferiority and are more likely to be rejected, so they must learn to cope with that and bounce back. Doing so is crucial to success and happiness, and instilling confidence at a young age helps set the individual up for life.

Tom is careful to distinguish between confidence and arrogance, and that's part of his messaging, too. "Sometimes, disabled children are very full of themselves and think that they're marvelous. They're not; they're like everybody else — no better, no worse. Some parents give their children an artificial confidence — it's not deep. And I think that this is because these children have always been boosted and praised and made to feel that they're special but they haven't failed. Every human being has to fail and they have to pick themselves up and realize 'I'm still okay.' Sometimes failure is horrible. Everybody fails, and just because you fail at this doesn't mean you're a failure at everything and it doesn't mean you're a bad person. And that's what I want to inculcate that you are okay even though you fail."

• • •

Apart from family, Tom's proudest achievement in his personal life is his friendships. He has a great capacity to make friends; he's very loyal to his friends, as they are to him. In his professional world, his proudest achievement is that people tell him that he makes them think.

Those six words — "different, but in a good way" — perfectly sum up Tom Shakespeare.

PATRICK FLANAGAN

Stroke play

Patrick is a student at University College Dublin
and is a swimmer training for the postponed
Tokyo 2020 Paralympic Games. He has spina bifida.

SITUATED ON THE NORTH ATLANTIC COAST of Ireland under the shadow of Benbulben Mountain on one side and Knocknarea Mountain on the other sits the village of Rosses Point in County Sligo. There the tide ebbs and flows on its three beaches: the short first beach, the very popular second beach, and the long isolated third beach. Just up from the beaches is the world-famous Rosses Point Golf Club founded in 1894. One of Ireland's great championship links courses, it follows the natural contours of this dune landscape. The course enjoys breathtaking views over mountains, sea, and green countryside — views immortalized in the poetry of W.B. Yeats, whose grave is only a few miles away.

Rosses Point has always been a special place for Patrick Flanagan, who is part of the well-known Flanagan golfing family that has played there for generations. Patrick's dad is a former Ireland team captain. Patrick's mother plays regularly; his grandmother also. His brothers have also played for Ireland, so making up a Flanagan family four-ball is never a problem.

Patrick was born into this golf-mad family in 1997 — the third of four children. Patrick has spina bifida. He grew up in Longford, a small rural town in the center of Ireland, where both parents were doctors. Though home during the week was in Longford, it was to their second home in Rosses Point that the family would retreat every possible weekend and holiday — answering the pull of a large extended family, the ocean, and golf. A few years ago, the family moved permanently to Rosses Point.

Patrick's parents were very keen for their son to take up a sport, but he found the "family game" didn't really suit him. "I did give golf a go for a while using splints and a Kaye walker and with a lot of support from my dad, but it just wasn't really a sport for me," he says.

Swimming was different, which he began at age eight. "Swimming was something I took to quite quickly — I was quite good in the water," he says. "It was my mum who spotted that early on. Mum used to bring us into the pool and she just encouraged me to float on my back. She was the one who first got me moving and comfortable in the water. She taught me to swim, and she got me to the stage that I was good enough to join the swimming club, and she encouraged me to do so. A few of my good friends in primary school were in the swimming club and they also encouraged me."

Swimming soon became a big part of Patrick's life. He says, "When I got in the water, I was as quick as anyone else. It didn't matter what my disability was; it didn't matter if I was kicking or not. It just mattered that I was beating the others down the length of the pool, which was fun to me — which is fun to any kid.

"I just kept going to the club. And then when I was about twelve, I kind of realized that it was something I really liked and I started taking it a bit more seriously. When I moved to secondary school, swimming wasn't a common sport — most of the lads there were playing football — but one of my good friends was still swimming. The two of us progressed together for the next few years. But the thing for me was that

I never really thought of myself as a swimmer with disability. It was just that I was a swimmer in the club with the other kids my age, the other guys. Obviously, as I got older, they got faster than me — that was always going to happen. But that never really bothered me, because I was still just there to train. I was still doing the same sessions that they were doing. I really just loved swimming.

"Swimming is just a perfect sport," he says, "because a person with almost any disability can get in the water."

• • •

Though sports were greatly encouraged in the family, academic and other interests were, too. Patrick attended primary and secondary schools in Longford and is currently finishing a degree in economics and finance at University College Dublin (UCD).

Music was also important. Outside of school he played classical violin, moving through all the grades and senior certificates, and piano to grade four or five. He and his younger brother also played in a youth orchestra that performed in concerts around Europe — Paris, Prague, Amsterdam, and Budapest. (With a modesty so typical of Patrick, he adds that his brother was a much better musician than he was.) In addition, in his last few years at secondary school, Patrick and a few friends played in a band called Caillte — the Irish word for "lost" — playing gigs in many tiny rural pubs.

When Patrick was growing up, he never considered his disability as much of a barrier. He says, "To some extent, I just followed what my siblings were doing. When you're younger, you don't really understand that you have a disability. You just kind of think that you're just a kid and this is just my wheelchair. You're not thinking 'Oh, those people see me as someone who has a disability." You don't have the understanding of that at that age, so it just seems like well, why not? I even tried sailing. I wonder what the instructors thought when they saw a guy in a wheelchair coming to do the two-week sailing course in Sligo in the summer. But it just never, ever fazed me. It just seemed logical. Why wouldn't I be able to do it?"

• • •

Patrick was about fourteen years old when he first got involved in Para swimming. "I so clearly remember my first session in Dublin," he says. "After about an hour and a half of continuous swimming, I got out of the water and started to get sick. I think it was a mixture of tiredness and nerves. But I still really enjoyed it. I still wanted to go back for the next one. And Mum was really good for encouraging me to continue."

Patrick recalls why Longford Swimming Club was so very important to his swimming career — apart from his friends being in the club. Before Patrick joined, the club already had a swimmer with a disability, which meant a pathway had already been established. On top of that, the club's head coach was really experienced and a very nice person.

It must have been the right package, because Longford Swimming Club has three members — one of them Patrick — potentially going to Tokyo for the postponed Paralympic Games.

Patrick also credits his siblings for their constant encouragement in his early swimming years. "They were there to support me. They knew when I had to be up early to be in the water at 5:30 a.m., and they were going to do that with me and drive me on the mornings I wasn't too keen. They would say, 'No, you're going to enjoy this. It will be worth it in the long run.' They all gave me that extra little push."

Once he began college, Patrick moved to the swimming club there, and in preparation for life post-college, he now trains with the National Aquatic Centre Swimming Club in Dublin.

• • •

Moving to competitive Para swimming meant being assigned to one of the categories within the Para swimming classification system. This classification isn't a perfect science, and it caused Patrick some early problems that weren't resolved until he was twenty.

Patrick is now an S6, but when he first started Para swimming he was incorrectly classified as an S8, which meant he was competing against people with less disability than him. Though swimming in a class that disadvantaged him, he still managed to pick up some medals at the junior level. At age fifteen, he was named Swim Ireland Disability Swimmer of the Year.

Patrick remembers his first big breakthrough. "When I was seventeen, I was reclassified as an S7, which was great. It gave me my first glimmer of hope of what I might be able to achieve in competitive Para swimming." It also coincided with his move to college, where he was successful in obtaining an elite sports scholarship.

Fortuitous for Patrick, a change in the classification system a couple of years later resulted in him being again reclassified as an S6, which he believes is the correct category for him. "I now get to compete against people with similar disabilities."

That same year he also made his senior debut at the European Championships. "That year the European Championships were held in Ireland, so unusually I was swimming in front of many home supporters, including a large contingent from Rosses Point, loudly cheering me on from the stands. The 400 meter freestyle was my main event. In the heats I came second, but in the final I was beaten to a medal position by a tenth of a second. I was absolutely gutted," he recalls.

Recovering from that disappointment took time. On reflection, he realizes that had he won a medal that day, he may not have had the huge hunger to relentlessly pursue qualification for Tokyo.

"The following year was a really good year for me," he says. "I swam a good race at the World Championships. I'd prefer to swim a good race and come sixth rather than come fourth and swim a bad race."

Finally, in January 2020, Patrick made the qualifying standard for Tokyo. He smiles, thinking of the moment: "That is the highlight of my career so far. I can remember turning around and seeing the clock and knowing that I was under the qualifying standard and that I was eligible to go. That's what you train your whole life for. And it's the best feeling ever."

Now that Patrick has made the qualification time, he is hopeful he will be part of the Irish Para swimming team traveling to Tokyo. The team will not be finalized until nearer the Games, but he has to continue his training regime as if the ticket is already in his back pocket. This is the uncertain life of competitive sport.

• • •

Patrick has always put a lot of emphasis on academics. "That's just because it's what I was encouraged to do," he says. "That's what my family did. Throughout school, I worked hard so that I could get into the degree I wanted." The program he selected at UCD — economics and finance — is among those with the highest academic entry requirements in Ireland.[1] "Ultimately, it was just down to the fact that math and accounting were my favorite subjects in school, and this degree is well recognized. It also helped that UCD has a fifty-meter swimming pool and a really good swim team."

Although the priority Patrick gives to academics is paramount, once he made the qualification time for the upcoming Paralympics he opted to take a break from his studies to focus on training — and then, a month later, the world interfered with those plans. COVID-19 became serious and the Paralympics were postponed to 2021.

Patrick has now returned to his studies, balancing the rigors of finishing college with a twenty-plus hour per week swim training regimen. "I learn so much about time management from balancing the two. If I'm getting up to go swimming in the pool at six o'clock in the morning, I can't stay up all night studying; I have to stay focused when I'm studying."

· · ·

Patrick's positive attitude to life and living with disability is part nature, part nurture. Certainly, his family's pragmatic attitude to disability has been fundamental. He says, "I used a Kaye walker and splints for most of primary school. It was kind of a deal with my parents that I would get to bring my wheelchair to school on a Friday — that was my treat. And I think everyone in the class thought that it was so cool for me to bring the wheelchair. I always preferred the wheelchair because I was faster. I had freedom, and I could keep up with things. I could play basketball on a Friday. Splints were so tough and such a hassle even to put on and off, and I used to have such problems with friction from them at my hips.

"I made the decision to use the wheelchair full time when I was about twelve and used it throughout secondary school. I just feel the wheelchair is much more natural. It gives me much more independence. It really is a societal belief that walking is better than being in a wheelchair, but it's not. For me a wheelchair is ten times better."

As Patrick has grown older he has come to appreciate his family's pragmatic attitude more: "In Para sport, you meet many people with different disabilities from different backgrounds, and with different attitudes to disability." He says he's noticed that many children with disabilities seem to be "bubble wrapped" and they're very cautious. His family's attitude was you've got to give everything a go, that you've got to try hard — that the limitation may be more a mental attitude than a physical limitation.

Patrick recognizes that his disability and experiences over the years have shaped his nature. "In primary school I hardly noticed my disability. I think maybe I started to notice it in secondary school — for example going to places with steps but no lift." Friends would often carry him into discos, much to the alarm of bouncers! And when going to friends' houses, he remembers he always had to stop and think, "Will there be an accessible toilet downstairs?"

Now that he's older he says, "I suppose you find more and more things come up, but you're more equipped to deal with them. Recently I was looking for accommodation in Dublin — on a student budget — and I was unable to find somewhere accessible. For me, I don't mind facing these issues, but for people with disabilities who might not be as comfortable, they can be a problem."

On competitiveness, he says, "Obviously, competing in Para swimming is a competitive endeavor, but I'm probably more competitive with myself than with other swimmers. Whether it's competitive or just being determined? I know what I want to do, and I just want to get it done."

Like many Para swimmers, Patrick believes that the classification system can be improved. "Your classification is everything, and if it's wrong, competitive Para swimming might be out of the question for you. In fairness, they're trying so hard to get it right, and they're constantly reviewing it. Like a lot of other sports, it relies on honesty among competitors. Some well-known Para swimmers, including Jessica Long, have spoken out in the media recently, which is the first step. Hopefully, it will be brought more into the limelight and it will improve over the next few years."

. . .

After college and his life in competitive swimming, Patrick envisions himself eventually entering the world of business. "My current ambition is to get to the Games in Tokyo and then I think a break will be lovely because for the last number of years, I barely have had any free time. You can imagine balancing that amount of training with academics. And after Tokyo I'm going to worry about my career and what I want to do after that.

"I'd like to be successful. I think that's just what drives me. I'd like to have success in whatever my professional career ends up being. I'd like to own my own business and be in a position of management; I think it's something I'd be good at doing. And I'd be proud of that."

He's deservedly proud now of both completing a tough degree and having qualified for and hopefully going to the Paralympics. As an old man, he hopes to be able to look down and see the Olympic rings on his arm. "I think this is especially because people don't expect that from someone who has a disability. It's just the way it is, unfortunately. I would love to surpass that expectation. I'd like, little by little, to change perceptions of what people with disabilities can achieve, what they're capable of. It's just to normalize disability."

Training during a pandemic for a yet unconfirmed slot in a postponed Games, while completing the last requirements of a challenging degree, is a true test of grit. Who knows where in the world life will take Patrick Flanagan. Regardless of what comes next, for Patrick, Rosses Point, on Ireland's North Atlantic coast — with his family, friends, and the ocean — will always exert a strong gravitational pull.

HARALDUR THORLEIFSSON

Master your craft, but don't forget to master your humanity.

Haraldur (Halli) is an Icelandic digital designer and founder of the company Ueno, which was bought by Twitter where he now works. He has muscular dystrophy.

ON ANY GIVEN NIGHT IN REYKJAVÍK, the capital of Iceland, street lights flicker on as the sun goes down. A warm glow showers the roads, illuminating the brightly painted orange and red houses below. As day turns to night, the central district comes alive. People pour onto two main streets, entering bars and restaurants that have been converted from old Icelandic homes.

Haraldur, "Halli," Thorleifsson grew up in the central district. That's where he would go out to meet friends, and where he first met his wife. Initially, Halli walked into those locales independently, but by the time he was in his mid-twenties, his leg muscles had weakened, and he started falling more often — requiring him to start using a wheelchair. Halli was born with muscular dystrophy, which meant that growing up, he had what he called a "funny walk."

"I started using a wheelchair when I was about twenty-six," says Halli. "I never used devices before, but I probably should have started using a wheelchair four or five years sooner than I did. I was getting very wobbly, and it was getting very hard for me to walk. I would fall quite a bit. That also started to create scenarios where I would avoid going out and doing things — I would just stay in the place that was comfortable.

"The freedom I experienced once I started using a wheelchair was pretty amazing."

The liberation that Halli experienced is an important part of his story: that a wheelchair often isn't restrictive or confining, but instead is a device that allows for greater freedom of movement. Becoming a wheelchair user had two effects on Halli's life: it granted him mobility, and it gave him stability when moving — thus avoiding falls. That stability, however, also helped enable the alcoholism he has since overcome, for now at least, he says.

Today, as a digital designer, Halli looks to improve user experiences with technology, much like he negotiates life as a wheelchair user. In 2014, he started his own agency, Ueno, which marries beautiful design with technology.

In a talk that Halli gave at the 2020 European conference of Figma, a tech company, he said: "Technology doesn't need to be just functional. I want to combine function and feeling in all of my work, because I believe in a future where technology makes people's lives better, where they feel connected and where they feel loved. I believe it's a future worth fighting for. I believe it's my job to do everything I can do to make that future become real."[1]

He recently started a fund with the mayor of Reykjavík, Dagur Eggertsson, supported by the president of Iceland, Guðni Jóhannesson, and the prime minister, Katrín Jakobsdóttir. The fund aims to make more local shops and restaurants wheelchair accessible. Given the old architecture in Reykjavík and the limited budget of many small businesses, the fund will be applied literally one ramp at a time.

"The idea is that we start a fund where we can pay for the ramps themselves," says Halli. "We can provide businesses with someone to draw up the plans, work with the city to approve changes to these old houses, and hire a construction company to build each ramp — fast. That's what we're launching."

In all that he does, Halli conveys a deep sense of empathy for others. In both his work and his side projects — like the new accessibility fund — he studies how people navigate life in unique ways, be it entering a restaurant or using technology. His drive, coupled with his relentless focus on producing high-quality work, started from humble beginnings.

• • •

Halli was born in Reykjavík in 1977. His parents were young, just twenty-two years old. At the time, his mom was a costume designer and generally extremely creative. His dad was an entrepreneur, running a small carpet-laying business with a handful of employees. Halli admits that saying he was inspired by his parents sounds nice — since he would later go on to pursue entrepreneurship and design — but he questions whether that's true. "I don't know what effect they had on me, but in a story arc that makes sense."

Halli grew up in a very safe and secure environment, and he has mostly positive memories of his childhood. Even though his parents weren't well off, he still had access to the same schools and health care as everyone else, which meant he didn't really notice any difference between himself and other kids.

Having access to the Scandinavian model of health care system helped.

"My parents realized that I had a disability when I was two years old," says Halli. "They noticed that I was walking on my toes quite a bit. I also started to walk later than other kids, although that wasn't the main clue."

At age three, Halli was diagnosed with muscular dystrophy. Later, when he was around age seven, doctors did a biopsy on his leg that confirmed the earlier diagnosis.

"The muscular dystrophy that I have is very slow progressing. I thought for a long time as a kid that the only thing that it affected was that I walked on my toes because my legs were shorter. We didn't talk about it a lot. Not that it was taboo; I just grew up thinking it didn't matter — pretty much to the point where I ignored it, as I have pretty much done my whole life."

Halli grew up mostly as an only child, with a half brother he didn't often see. His parents partied a lot when Halli was young, though Halli only remembers them as loving parents.

"My dad was an alcoholic. He got sober when I was ten. I don't remember him drinking, even though he apologizes for it a lot now," says Halli. "He and my mom were always wonderful parents. They split up when I was young, so I don't remember them together. Both of them found other partners and I don't remember them without those partners. So, I grew up with two families. There was a lot of love, which was good."

When Halli was eleven, his world changed. His mom died in a car accident, and he remembers the major impact it had on him. "When my mom died, my personality changed quite a bit," says Halli. "I went into myself a lot more."

The pain of his mom's death was, like his disability, something Halli chose to ignore. The grief he repressed at the time came back later as a void — one he acknowledges now, many years later. Before dealing with that pain and grief in his thirties, there were years of ups and downs — the high highs of massive professional success, and the low lows of alcoholism.

• • •

After Halli finished high school, he enrolled at the University of Iceland with grand plans to study constructional engineering — a plan that lasted three days. He switched majors and graduated instead with a dual degree in philosophy and finance. While at university, he started to work in digital design, something he thought he'd do for a bit while he decided his career path.

One day, he saw a job posting in New York for Cuban Council, an agency he admired, and he decided to apply. Even though he had been outside the country only a handful of times — and never to New York — he decided to move abroad when he was offered the job.

Halli was twenty-nine years old when he began this new job — but it didn't last. By this time he had started drinking heavily. He attributes his drinking to many factors, including the alcoholism in his family, and that he never dealt with his mom's death.

"I was only in New York for about a year," says Halli. "I got into a lot of bad habits for which I rightly got fired."

Halli moved back to Iceland after losing his job and began freelancing, which he continued to do for the next several years. When he was thirty-four, he stopped drinking and married his girlfriend, whom he had been dating for a couple of years. One year later, their daughter was born and Halli made another brave move.

• • •

As a freelancer, he had the freedom to work remotely and travel, and in 2012, he moved with his family to Japan. While there, he had his biggest professional breakthrough — leading the team to design Google's first Santa Tracker, which used Google Maps technology to help kids follow Santa as he travels around the globe on Christmas Eve.

Halli poured everything into that project — hiring a team of designers and overdelivering on the brief from Google. In the process, he created an entire digital universe visited by millions of children worldwide.

"The project got a fair amount of attention, but mostly it gave me confidence — that I could take on projects and successfully deliver them. It showed me that I could pull together teams and do a lot of the things that are required to start my own agency," says Halli.

Halli's freelance journey continued alongside his world travels for the next year. He stayed in Airbnbs as his family moved to Canada, the U.S., Brazil, Spain, and Argentina. And then exactly one year after launching the Google Santa Tracker, while he was in Argentina with his family, he did take that big step to start his own agency. It was Christmas Day, and he talked with his wife about a name for the new venture.

Ueno.

One of their favorite places in Tokyo was a park named Ueno, similar to the Spanish word for good, *bueno*, but without the *b*. Halli liked how it looked: it had four letters, plus it had a nice sound.

Halli dove in, completely devoting himself to his new enterprise. He was relentless, working one-hundred-hour weeks, and after just one year, his agency was established and very successful.

Reflecting on that first year, Halli has said, "I learned that I could do pretty much anything I set my mind to. That . . . confidence is what has carried me through a lot of hard times.

"It's worth noting here that I am not an advocate of 'hustle culture.'[2] This type of lifestyle can have very serious long-term effects on people . . . It was a huge sacrifice, not only for me but for my family. My wife made this possible and I owe her everything."[3]

Over the next five years, Ueno grew fast, opening offices in Iceland, New York, Los Angeles, and San Francisco. Along the way, Halli remained committed to the agency's culture, making sure that he and his team were thoughtful about every piece of work and the positive impact they could have with their growing success.

At the end of 2020, Halli tweeted a powerful statement about disability in tech: "I am 43 years old. I have been in design and tech for over 20 years. I have had thousands and thousands of meetings in my career.

"Not once, in all that time, have I been in a professional meeting with another person in a wheelchair . . . Representation of people with disabilities in my field is fairly close to zero. And to be honest I don't really see any allies discussing this fact."[4]

Halli has often used Twitter to highlight this massive gap in the industry. When he tweeted "Who are some of your favorite people with disabilities in product design leadership?" his followers replied with just a handful of names — which to Halli was "not surprising but still heartbreaking."[5] He laments the lack of early opportunities available to people with a disability.

"There are very few people with disabilities in tech. I think this gets lost," says Halli. "There's rightly a huge focus on gender, on Black and Brown, on Latinx. There are a lot of areas that get a lot of focus, very rightfully and deservedly so. But I don't think that proportionately people with disabilities get nearly the same kind of focus. They're by far the most disenfranchised group, the least paid — and much more likely to experience homelessness.

"There's a need to bring in more people with disability into the *creation* of tech. A surprising number of things get made that people can't use. I think that's because there's nobody with disability at the table. I don't think we can fix it if people with disabilities aren't there, because you have to live it to really appreciate it."

Halli believes the lack of people with disabilities working in tech is a problem that needs to be addressed much earlier, especially in the U.S. where people aren't given equal opportunities. He notes that people with disabilities often face many problems — such as unequal access to education, health care, and social experiences — which in turn make them less competitive in the job market.

"There's a huge group of people that we turn into 'patients' — not because of their disability or because of their situation, but because of how society is set up. They're never given the path to success, however they define their own success," says Halli.

· · ·

In January 2021, Halli posted a blog titled "24,895 hours later." In it, he announced that Ueno was being acquired by Twitter, saying, "I'm proud we are able to leave on a high note. I feel like we won the agency game and there were no more things to prove . . . I'm proud we are able to end the story with a happy ending."[6]

With his success in design and tech, the upward slope of Halli's impact is steep and not slowing down any time soon.

Having sold Ueno to Twitter, Halli feels a major sense of relief having stepped aside from the CEO role. As an employee at Twitter now, he is no longer the person that ultimately has all the responsibility. And despite the acquisition and shiny industry awards, he sees his greatest accomplishment as his two children — nine-year-old Emma and four-year-old Miro. In parenting, Halli takes a thoughtful approach in how he leads.

"We try to give them a lot of freedom," says Halli. "We'd much rather have them break a leg than not experiment. We try to teach them to be respectful, while still making sure that they don't lose sight of themselves."

Halli is a role model for his children, although he questions his own reasons for success — he strives to prove to himself and others that he's capable of doing high-quality work. He battles with a feeling of being inferior, and while he admits that's not the healthiest source of motivation, he tries to channel it in ways that leave a positive impact.

"I think successful people have something in them that they have to prove," says Halli. "They have a hole in their soul that they can't fill. Part of why I have to continue doing these things is because I have a broken image of myself that I constantly need to disprove.

"I think the hole comes partly from my disability. There's an inherent feeling of being less for a lot of people with disabilities. Even if you don't mentally agree with it, it is something that seeps in through society. For me, it definitely has an impact — where I feel maybe my disability is an issue, but I can show you that I can do other things really well."

Halli acknowledges that it's different to have an event that changes your life versus being born with a disability that is always there. In his experience, he never had a moment of reckoning that pushed him to deal with his disability. By ignoring it for years, he never really processed it.

But Halli *is* starting that process of dealing with his disability now. He has tweeted that "Until recently, I would never post a photo on any platform of me in a wheelchair. The reasons are complicated and I'm not even sure I understand them all myself yet. But I know shame is a big factor. Shame of my body and my weakness." Days later, he tweeted a photo of himself in his wheelchair alongside his son and the president of Iceland. By giving visibility to his disability, he is publicly learning how to overcome the shame he has felt for years, becoming a leader for others who battle similar feelings of inferiority.

Together, Halli, the president, the prime minister, and the mayor have made impressive progress on the new accessibility fund, raising almost $500,000 to date to support his plan to build one hundred ramps in the next year.

Whether designing ramps or technology, Halli is purposeful about "creating moments of connection," which was the title of that keynote speech he gave at the Figma conference. He left his audience with this message, reflecting his personal credo: "Master your craft, but don't forget to master your humanity. Do what you can to make the world better through your work."[1]

CATHRYN GRAY

Together we can make a difference

Cathryn is a student at the University of Michigan and a track-and-field athlete. She has spastic diplegia.

CATHRYN GRAY'S RADIANT SMILE, framed by her dark brown hair and warm eyes, has a way of drawing you in. Her tone of familiarity gives you the impression that you already know her, even if you can't quite place how you first met. And when Cathryn talks, she radiates positivity.

That spirit of optimism is what she hopes to spread far and wide — among both people living with and without disabilities.

When Cathryn was born in 2000, she was immediately diagnosed with cerebral palsy (CP). The doctors told her parents that her condition came with a strict canon of limitations — and that she would never walk, talk, or live a normal life.

Thankfully, for Cathryn, her parents didn't listen.

"My parents are my heroes," she says. "I owe my life to them. When they were told my life outcome would be grim, their response was 'No, you don't know what she's capable of yet. Don't sell her short.'"

But that didn't make the years that followed her diagnosis easy, for either Cathryn or her parents. The extensive treatment she needed throughout childhood — including years of physical therapy and three orthopedic surgeries at age six, eight, and thirteen — kept her isolated from her peers. Although essential, the treatment proved to be a lonely experience.

Overall, the surgeries helped, but they took a toll. The second one was especially tough, as it failed. "That was a really hard time," Cathryn says. "It was very mentally difficult. But I was blessed with parents who kept believing in me, always encouraging me to persist."

At age thirteen, Cathryn had her final surgery, a foot reconstruction and tendon lengthening. "I still have scars on my left foot, which have healed, and in a good way they're a reminder of what I've been through and how far I've come. They are not just reminders of the physical ordeal, but also of the hard work I've had to invest in my long-term recovery."

Cathryn jokes that the process should be called "surgery plus rehab," because the surgery is the easy part — it's the long, intense period of rehab afterwards that challenges a person. At times, physical therapy felt like a looming cloud. The constant reminders from the specialists about the importance of doing the exercises could be hard. It is only in retrospect that she could see the benefit. "It really taught me how if you work for something, and you stick with a goal, the outcome is really, really great. But you have to put in the work and you have to put in the time."

Through all the surgeries and years of physical therapy, Cathryn developed the tenets she lives by today: a strong work ethic, dedication and perseverance in everything she does. Those tenets continue to guide her as she climbs the ranks in the world of international adaptive track and field.

• • •

Cathryn grew up in an athletic family in Atlanta, Georgia. Her dad coached her older sister's soccer team, and her mom encouraged both girls to try a wide variety of sports. Knowing that sports would benefit Cathryn's muscles, her mom, Cynthia, signed the girls up for lessons in rock climbing, ballet, kayaking, tennis, T-ball, soccer — you name it. Whatever the sport, Cynthia would say, "You're doing it!"

The type of cerebral palsy that Cathryn has is spastic diplegia. This makes her physically weaker, but not without the ability to keep at whatever athletic endeavor put in front of her, especially with her mom cheering her on. In the harder moments, when Cathryn would fall down during physical therapy or at school, Cynthia was relentless about encouraging Cathryn not to pity herself, to get back up and walk it off. It was a tough love that was hard to stomach in the moment, but it was an approach Cathryn learned to appreciate in the long run.

Cynthia was also devoted to Cathryn's treatments, going with her to every therapy appointment and dedicating whole summers to physical therapy before surgeries. She took the reins, challenging recommendations for drastic and severe surgeries. She taught Cathryn how to advocate for herself with doctors.

More daunting, at times, was being treated as different by other kids. Cathryn's cerebral palsy does not affect her cognitively, but her childhood peers didn't understand that.

"I was bullied throughout elementary school and middle school. Really badly," says Cathryn. "But my mom would always say, 'Don't listen to what they say; you're more than your disability.'"

Cynthia prioritized family dinnertime, asking Cathryn about what she was learning in school to prepare her academically and to encourage her to form her own opinions. Those dinners also gave Cathryn a chance to connect with her sister, Ally, a relationship she especially cherishes. Having a sister who was two years older gave Cathryn an early role model and advocate. Ally always stuck up for Cathryn when kids at school picked on her. And she showed Cathryn what was possible in sport, pushing her to do her best.

"One of the best things about my childhood that I really value is that my family never viewed me in a separate category because of my disability," Cathryn says. "I think that's really important, because although I was getting bullied in school, I knew home was my safe space. I had a great support system, and I always knew I was loved and accepted.

"Not everyone has parents that are as involved as my mom is in cerebral palsy advocacy and nonprofit work."

• • •

By the time Cathryn was thirteen, she still hadn't landed on a sport she felt passionate about, one that would stick. It was her mom who first suggested she try adaptive track and field, but Cathryn was initially dismissive.

"I looked at her, and I laughed. I was wearing an ankle-foot orthosis at the time and doing exercises to get stronger after surgery," says Cathryn. "I said, 'that's not a possibility.' I didn't think I could run. I'd never seen a female adaptive track-and-field athlete. I didn't see anyone like me who could run and could throw. I didn't have anyone to look up to."

But with the "try anything" attitude Cathryn had been brought up with, she signed up. As it has turned out, track and field is the last sport she tried — she loved it immediately and never looked back.

Cathryn started adaptive track and field and met her first coach, who also coached the high school team she would later join. She tried multiple events, eventually deciding on running and throwing the discus, javelin, and shot put. It opened up a whole new world to her — prior to that experience, she didn't even know how to run.

"What I love about track and field is that when I'm running or throwing, I'm completely free from anything that happened during the day," says Cathryn. "I feel the most fulfilled when I'm competing. Sports have changed my life."[1]

It wasn't just the physical benefits of sports that nurtured Cathryn; socially and academically, she also began to thrive.

Within the adaptive sports community, she was surrounded by other athletes with physical disabilities, and she discovered the value of community. That community gave her the confidence to join her high school track-and-field team, something she had been reluctant to do because she was the only member with a physical disability. After being bullied in elementary and middle school, she worried the petty comments about her gait would follow her to high school. Fortunately, the bullying stopped. Her peers — athletes without disabilities — embraced her and were entirely supportive, creating a culture of acceptance and inclusion. (Cathryn and her mom, Cynthia, successfully lobbied the State of Georgia to change the rules — to allow students with disabilities to compete on their high school track-and-field teams for the very first time. Together, they paved the way for equal opportunity and participation.)

Finding her confidence in sports also helped her flourish in high school. Cathryn excelled academically, earning straight As in subjects ranging from Latin to computer science, including in six advanced placement classes. As well, she volunteered more than two thousand service hours and was a leader among her peers — being elected as choir president and to homecoming court, and named as prom queen.[2]

Cathryn's influence began to spread across Atlanta and even nationwide. She was named one of the sixteen outstanding high school seniors in Atlanta, and Positive Female Athlete for the State of Georgia in 2020. She earned a series of awards, including a Women's Sports Foundation grant, in addition to scholarships from Coca-Cola, Heisman, and Microsoft.

All of these accolades led Cathryn to extend her voice and impact, ultimately connecting her with even more advocates for adaptive sports. One of those groups is GLASA, the Great Lakes Adaptive Sports Association, a Paralympic team that has been a transformative experience for her. Again, being surrounded by people like her makes a world of difference.

"If you have a physical disability, it's really important to have a community that supports you," says Cathryn.

With that community support behind her, Cathryn excelled. She went on to win three state championship titles in track and field — in the 100 meters, shot put, and discus. She was named a U.S. Paralympic High School All-American three times — the only female in Georgia selected. And then more: growing up, she never imagined there could be a pathway to represent the United States in international competition, but that's exactly what she would go on to do.

· · ·

Sant Cugat sits inland from Barcelona in the northeastern corner of Spain. Romanesque and Gothic buildings dating back to the ninth century line the town center, where a blend of foreign languages can be heard among visitors to the small borough of ninety thousand people. Lush, green trees and expansive fields surround the village, immersing the peaceful

Spanish countryside with little thought to the giant metropolis of Barcelona just twenty kilometers away.

Among the series of expansive fields sits the High Performance Sports Center of Catalonia, built in 1992 to support the Olympic Games in Barcelona. In summer 2018, the Sports Center served as the main venue of the CP World Games, an event that would change Cathryn's life. Delegations from twenty-five countries traveled to Spain, with one thing in common — they all had cerebral palsy. There, Cathryn competed on the U.S. team, comprising twelve athletes ranging in age from thirteen to twenty-four.

The Games showed Cathryn that cerebral palsy is worldwide. What especially struck her was not only seeing how broad the cerebral palsy community is, but also, how unifying. She traded pins[3] with athletes from Scotland, Ireland, and even Russia, and thought to herself, "Where have you been all my life?"

"When I was younger, I was definitely ashamed and nervous to admit that I had cerebral palsy," says Cathryn. "I didn't know how people would perceive me. Cerebral palsy could be very isolating. But when we got to Spain, I thought, this is so cool — all of us in the same area all at once."

In Spain she found a unique connection that had been missing when she was a child. Although Cathryn had had fantastic physical therapists, they only knew so much about cerebral palsy, since it's often not a focus of their training. At adaptive sports competitions like the CP World Games, Cathryn could identify with people on a deeper level, because she knew what they were going through.

She felt immense pride representing her country, wearing the U.S. uniform, wanting to make a good impression. "I want to show others not to count us out just because we have a disability," says Cathryn. "I want to show that we have something to give. The medals are great, but I like the team aspect even more. I like getting to know people's stories. I want people to be able to share. Because of people's lack of understanding of disability, they might be quick to pity that person or dismiss their opinion.

"I feel lucky that in sport, I found my voice."

• • •

Today, at the age of twenty, Cathryn is ranked fourth in the world in her classification in both javelin and discus, and tenth in the world in shot put. She is a freshman at the University of Michigan, a university that is changing the game for people with disabilities. When selecting where to study, she considered other programs at the University of Texas at Arlington and Arizona State University, which also have adaptive sports programs. The pull to attend the University of Michigan was threefold: the perfect blend of athletics, academics, and advocacy. "One of the things that attracted me to Michigan was the adaptive sports program, because it's just starting out," says Cathryn. "I feel really blessed to be able to help the program grow. This new University of Michigan adaptive team is making a bigger impact than we know."[4]

There, Cathryn is a pioneer: the first female adaptive athlete on scholarship at the university, and a founding member of the university's first adaptive track-and-field program.[5] That's a massive achievement in a university that's a powerhouse in collegiate sports.[6]

In Michigan, she now has a bigger microphone. And with that mic, she has ambitions to inspire others. "It's been a long but really rewarding journey. I'm glad I have the opportunity to speak now, because I think representation for people with disabilities is so important," says Cathryn.

One critical component of representation that Cathryn prioritizes is sharing her personal experience of being a woman with a physical disability. She finds that women with disabilities have an extra layer of pressure. "It takes more work because we're already burdened by gender stereotypes," says Cathryn. "You feel like you don't have a place in the world. A lot of the women with cerebral palsy around me get really down on themselves because of that extra burden. It can make it harder to try new things."

The desire to try new things still drives Cathryn, especially when people underestimate her abilities. Those low expectations placed on her since birth serve as huge motivation. She is on a quest to prove others wrong, to show that she can achieve great things, despite her cerebral palsy. She is critical of the tendency to put people with cerebral palsy into a box because of their disability. As her mom told her from day one, living with cerebral palsy is only a fraction of who Cathryn is — it affects her life, but it's not all of her.

After graduation, Cathryn hopes to become a lawyer and advocate for others, using her experiences with disability and the medical system. It is her life's mission to give hope to others like her.

For Cathryn, building a career in law has a lot to do with helping children. Some of Cathryn's fondest memories at track-and-field competitions are of helping at youth clinics, where she has seen how smart and empathetic young children are. Because of their physical disability, Cathryn says, many children notice *everything*, since they themselves are put under a microscope from a very young age. She wants to tap into that strong intuition that children have, to let them know they're not alone, that their voices deserve to be heard too.

Cathryn's legacy is already impressive. And she's only getting started. "All we people with disabilities really want is to be included," she says. "I want people with cerebral palsy to know that they're not alone; people care about you. My advice is to stick with it. It's okay to ask for help. If you're willing to ask, for the most part people are willing to help you. I don't know where I would be without sport. Once I found my communities, I knew I'll be in them for life, because my life is going to lead down the path of advocacy.

"I want to be the role model I never had: a person with a disability showing others what is possible.

"Together we can make a difference."

ROBIN BARNETT

The color purple

Robin is a career diplomat and former
British ambassador to Romania, Poland,
and Ireland. He has hemiplegia.

THE DATE IS DECEMBER 3, 2019, and the location is the British Embassy, in Dublin, Ireland. Ambassador Robin Barnett is at the podium dressed in a purple shirt and tie to deliver a speech to mark International Day of Persons with Disabilities. The backdrop, with the words "British Embassy Dublin" and the royal arms, is also colored purple.

Robin Barnett, British ambassador to Ireland from 2016 to 2020, has hemiplegia, a type of cerebral palsy. It affects the right side of his body. On this day, he tells the audience, "There are an estimated one billion people living with disabilities worldwide — indeed, I am one of them."[1]

An ambassador at the podium delivering a speech is pretty usual. An ambassador at the podium delivering a speech about disability from lived experience is very unusual.

What's even more unusual is that Robin didn't learn he had cerebral palsy until age sixty.

"I was attending an event with a VIP, and a young girl of about nine or ten with cerebral palsy came onto the stage and put up a slide. It showed the three main types of cerebral palsy. She was number one. I was transfixed by number three — hemiplegia. This was when I learned that I have cerebral palsy. Everything in the third picture was me.

"A well-known figure sitting next to me said, 'You've aged about fifty years in two minutes, what's happened?' Because

I trust this guy implicitly, I said, 'I just discovered that I have cerebral palsy.'

"It was a big shock."

By this time, Robin's parents were both deceased, so he couldn't ask them about it. His father had died suddenly when he was just eleven, and it was shortly after that he had his last significant conversation with his mother about his disability. "I think the terms 'hemiplegia' and 'spastic' might have been used," he says, but up to the point when that young girl spoke, he had no knowledge that his disability was a type of cerebral palsy.

With his discovery, he visited his doctor to learn more. Cerebral palsy is usually diagnosed in childhood by a pediatrician, and as that was clearly not an option for Robin at age sixty, his doctor sent him to a neurologist.

Of that visit, Robin says, "We had a great chat. He told me that the medical advice I had been given all those years ago — that whatever this is, is not going to get any better or worse — was totally sound, but that it was scandalous that they hadn't told me what it was."

The one piece of advice the neurologist left him with was to keep his weight under control. He took that seriously, and worked to lose a significant amount of weight by deliberately eating less and exercising more (walking twenty thousand steps daily). He says of the result, "I feel much better; I like my new self-image." And he is quick to pass on the same advice to others: if you're disabled, the last thing you can afford is to be overweight.

• • •

Robin grew up in southern England. He has one sister who is six years younger.

"I think my parents were always aware that there was some kind of physical problem. From very early on, I walked on my toes on my right side. It also became increasingly apparent that my left side grew very much better than my right. In later years, if I put a watch on my left wrist it would need a much bigger strap than one on my right.

"It became apparent quite quickly that I wasn't physically capable of doing everything that everybody else could, and the complex part, I think, was I knew I was different.

"We spent a number of years working with medical professionals. The first really sensible thing they did was to put a very heavy plaster on my right leg for half a year, with weekly visits back for adjustments.

"I have a limp — my right leg is two inches shorter than my left, but I can put my heel down to the ground on my right side."

When Robin was about five, medical professionals strongly suggested he try swimming. "We didn't have a lot of money, but my parents scraped together enough to go to an outdoor swimming pool at a hotel near where we lived. In winter, they couldn't afford for me to go to an indoor pool, so I was allowed to go to a medical swimming pool."

Robin remembers the other children there, many without limbs, and likely affected by the drug thalidomide. "Even at that age I was just about smart enough to realize that, yes, I had problems, but by comparison, I had no problems at all. That was a very crucial moment for me."

Over the next few years, he had periodic meetings with a specialist. "My condition got neither better nor, very importantly, worse. It was stable," he says. Then, when he was eleven, a visit to new specialist — a surgeon — presented him with two treatment choices. The first was to do a procedure on his good left leg. The surgeon bluntly explained what it would mean: "By cutting into your left leg and making it shorter, it will balance you up somewhat, but it does have a drawback — your good leg will never be quite as good once we've cut a piece out." The second, the surgeon said, was "a new technique where we could have you in bed for six months and we'll try stretching your right leg and see what that does for you."

By implication only, there was a third option — to do nothing. He and his mother took the third option.

This was the last real conversation he had with his mother about his disability. He says her very practical attitude seemed to be to ignore it and just "get on with it." He wonders, now, whether she should have talked with him about it more, or whether he should have asked more questions. But he emphasizes that she was a steadfast and important supporter over the years. He explains, "Some parents think they know what you should be; they tell you, and they expect you to go ahead and do it and fulfill *their* dreams, not yours. My mum never ever did that. She asked intelligent questions, she was always supportive and interested. Basically, her approach was to give me an occasional shove — for example, when I didn't feel like writing an essay — but otherwise she let me get on with it. I mean that in a really positive sense. My mum was a crucial and hugely positive influence."

After choosing to "do nothing," he says, "the health system kind of lost interest. I was quite glad that I was no longer going backwards and forwards to specialists."

Robin in no way attributes any blame to anyone for any of this; he's just recounting how things were as he was growing up in England in the sixties and seventies.

In school, he always had one or two friends, but says, "It was tough. Kids are cruel; a few were deliberately so, the vast majority accidentally." It wasn't unusual for him to hear the kids saying, "Here comes hop-along."

"I did feel different, but most of all I felt frustrated that I couldn't join in with sport," he says. "I love football and it's something I would have loved to have been good at playing. But most teachers decided quite quickly that it was much easier to let me do what I wanted during a games lesson."

One early teacher, Clive Harrison, stands out for Robin for his kindness. "He was a history teacher, but his passion was cricket, and when he realized I couldn't play, he decided to make me into a cricket umpire, saying, 'I need a second umpire.' I asked if I could borrow his umpiring book because my mother could never have afforded to buy me a copy. That teacher bought me my own copy."

To this day, Robin remains appreciative of that cricket master, and he kept up cricket umpiring into adulthood, when his work on Foreign Office assignments allowed.

• • •

In his early years at secondary school, Robin was, by his own description, "introverted, shy, and quite self-conscious." He remembers being sixteen, "coming to that age where the opposite sex was interesting but my self-image was really difficult. I was the guy with the limp. I was never going to be the cool guy everyone wanted to go onto the disco floor with."

He started to come into his own when he went to a Sixth Form College — a college specifically for the final two years of secondary school — where he completed A levels. "It was much more like university than school," he says.

"A friend signed me up for a course in improvisation — basically drama without the script. That didn't fit with introverted, nervous me, but my friend just put my name down. For some reason I didn't challenge him. That was the beginning of a very long journey to evolve myself from being somebody who was very self-conscious to someone who was able to do things in public. I performed in a rock-and-roll musical. I started debating — I famously spoke in a debate about the 1975 EU referendum, though I wasn't old enough to vote in it. People told me that I was very good.

"I suddenly realized that I could talk, and that maybe I could do this public thing."

Robin went from Sixth Form College to the University of Birmingham, studying law. There, he was active in drama and student politics, being elected to the Guild of Students (students' union).

"Over the years I moved from being an introvert to being a learned extrovert. That meant that my career choices would be a bit different," he says. "One day while perusing books at the university's careers office, it suddenly struck me that I wanted to work abroad. That was the one moment of revelation in my life, and after that I never ever had a doubt about the work I wanted to do."

Eighteen months later, Robin joined the Foreign and Commonwealth Office.

• • •

With that decision to work abroad, Robin began a single-minded pursuit of his dream — which took longer than he had hoped because of a recruitment freeze put in place when Prime Minister Margaret Thatcher came to power.

But he was resolute: "I turned down a better paying job in the bank, without having an absolute guarantee of joining the Foreign Office."

Even the setback of failing his medical — because of his disability — didn't stop him. "That was the first time that my disability became an issue," he says. He appealed the decision, and won.

Robin joined the Foreign Office in 1980 in a junior desk job looking after Indonesia and the Philippines. Colleagues were kind to him about his disability. "Every now and again people, including senior people, would ask me, 'Are we walking too fast, shall we get a cab?' I always answered 'No, thank you.' After a while, to make life easier for everyone, I suggested reversing things, saying, 'If I think I'm being asked to do something that's a bit physically difficult, I will tell you.'"

He soon learned that the effect of him telling a few people to ignore his disability meant that it became a nonissue, and his self-confidence grew. "I wasn't the life and soul of a party, but I got better and better and I could hold my own in meetings."

Working at the Foreign Office, Robin got the chance to learn a language and chose Polish. He had been fascinated about Poland since childhood when he read *The Silver Sword*, by Ian Serraillier, about Polish children in World War II, and later from learning about life there from a Polish teacher in Sixth Form College.

That led to Robin's first overseas posting — in Poland — and the start of realizing his dream of working abroad.

After three years, he was brought back to London, then moved to Vienna, and then to the United Nations in Manhattan, where the work often involved long meetings into the small hours, but his disability never caused any lack of stamina. In fact, his disability rarely presented as a problem at all. When he returned to work in London covering the Balkans, he had to take many trips by helicopter, which is not an easy craft for a person with disability to get in and out of. On the rare occasion it was problematic, "I would just turn to someone from the military and ask for help," he says.

A later role in London running the UK visa-issuing operation, a global operation with three and a half thousand staff based in about two hundred countries, is where he says he really learned about people and change management. He credits the team there for working hard to bring focus on customer service. Issues such as the inaccessibility of old buildings for people with disabilities, for example, came to the fore.

Robin's next appointment was as British ambassador to Romania, and that's when he "came out" about his disability. Up to then, he had always tried to keep it very low key, and as much as possible have everyone ignore it. But in Romania, he realized what he could achieve for others by being very open about his disability as an ambassador. He has said of that time, "It occurred to me the amount of good I could do for showing people I was able to have a good career and my disability had never stood in the way. I found this was extremely important to me — to send that message to those that needed to hear it."[2]

Robin thought deeply about how to advance the message about disability, but also about minorities in general. He recruited senior politicians to play table tennis with people with disabilities. "Some of the politicians were absolutely great, and the image of senior Romanian politicians being slaughtered in the nicest possible way by people with serious disabilities was brilliant."

He talked with journalists about how it felt to read the results of a study that showed how "a very large percentage of

Romanians would rather not work with a disabled person in their workplace."

He convened groups of role models to tell their stories. "As ambassador, being able to put a whole load of folks into a room to tell their stories is incredibly powerful."

From that point on, it was a priority for Robin to be a role model for people with a disability.

• • •

Robin was appointed ambassador to Poland in 2011. "This was for me the Holy Grail," he says. "I remember telling my mother about it. At this time, she was very feeble and died soon after, but I was able to tell her and she definitely understood that I'd achieved my life's ambition. It was very special."

Taking up his position in Poland, Robin found that the ambassador's office had already been doing quite a lot of work on disability. The 2012 London Paralympic Games were coming up, so he became very involved with the Polish Paralympic team. "I got to know a lot of very fine Polish Paralympians." Because of work commitments, Robin wasn't able to attend the Paralympics in London or see coverage on TV, but he made a speech at the Paralympic team's send-off. That team won thirty-six medals.

Robin's final posting in 2016 was as ambassador to Ireland, and he retired in 2020. A year before, and forty years after graduating with his bachelor degree, he returned to his alma mater to be awarded an honorary doctorate in law.

• • •

Today Robin lives in Poland with his Polish partner. He has two sons and two grandchildren. He continues to work on making a difference for people living with disabilities.

"I want to learn how to become a more helpful role model — we never stop learning." For example, he has learned that sometimes you can be too good at disguising the complexities of living life with a disability, and people's expectations of you become too high. That was brought home to him one day when, to avoid tripping, he moved close to a person, who then felt threatened. Robin asked, "Do you not see that I'm disabled?" The person answered, "I just thought you had a gammy leg or something."

Another time a friend commented to him that he noticed how good he was at putting his socks on with one hand, saying that he couldn't do that himself. Robin replied, "Well, I can't use two hands to put on my socks — I have no choice."

It's those sometimes subtle effects of disability that people aren't aware of. "It takes me a lot longer to get dressed than most people," he said, and that adds to the time it takes to do the ordinary activities of daily living.

Robin believes one of the big issues that very often hinders people with disabilities is their self-perception. "Sometimes, it's your self-perception that is the biggest obstacle to success. When I think about my career, it involved walking into rooms full of people, often as the host. If you had told me at the age of fifteen that I would be doing that successfully for a living, I would have told you that you were crazy."

Thinking of the Paralympians he has met, he notes that many are fitter, faster, and better than their Olympian colleagues because they put the effort in. "They're motivated, they have the stamina." This is an important message for everyone.

"People with disability need to be willing to put themselves forward for a job. Often they don't because they lack confidence or they worry that they won't be supported enough to do the job once they get it.

"Those of us with disability need to recognize that if we want to achieve something, it's not all about other people helping us achieve it. It's not that I don't recognize that help and reasonable adjustments may be needed, but a big part of it is us," he says.

He acknowledges that being able to reach out to somebody and ask for help is also important. In fact, he's had a reminder of that lesson himself recently, when he broke a finger on his better hand, which meant he had to ask for help with daily activities.

For others in the workforce, his message is, "As a colleague, as an employer of people with disabilities, you need to cast aside all your preconceptions."

At the time of writing, the world was in the midst of the COVID-19 pandemic, which highlighted a particular challenge for people with disabilities because, as Robin points out, "a lot of people who have a disability also have mental health issues. People's mental health has suffered a great deal as a consequence of COVID. Some of the routine care for people with disabilities has suffered. COVID is particularly evil because it manages to find ways of being particularly difficult for those who most need help from the broad health system."

Always in pursuit of learning, it leaves him to wonder, "How can we support people who are in these very difficult situations? Who knows, one day we could get another COVID — what lessons can we learn from this?"

• • •

In his speech to honor International Day of Persons with Disabilities, Robin explained why he was wearing purple. "The color purple has been increasingly associated with disability symbolizing a new narrative about the contribution of disabled people in the workforce and the wider community."[1]

After the event, he added, "Seeing the embassy lit in purple and hearing from inspirational speakers . . . touched everyone present. It demonstrated that whatever differences there are between us, as people we all dream and aspire to be the best that we can."[3]

TANNI GREY-THOMPSON

Aim high, even if you hit a cabbage

Tanni is a member of the UK House of Lords
and a retired Paralympic wheelchair racer.
She has spina bifida.

HOLDING HER DAUGHTER, Carys, in her lap, Baroness Tanni Grey-Thompson ("Tanni"), DBE,[1] poses for a photo. Her eyes crinkle as she smiles, sitting surrounded by green grass and wearing short sleeves, enjoying the warmth of the day in the summer of 2004. The child's short blonde hair is cut neatly, framing her face. Her joy is ebullient: a toothy, toddler grin with eyes shut tight in excitement, hands clenched in fists. In Tanni's left hand, her gold wedding band shines as she grips the trio of Paralympic tickets.

Carys was just two years old when Tanni competed in the Athens 2004 Paralympic Games, her fifth and final Games. Carys watched in the stands, wearing a white T-shirt sporting the emphatic words "Go Mammy!!" Tanni won two gold medals at those Games, and after each medal ceremony, she celebrated with her daughter and husband, Ian. And each time, Carys's fingers reached to the top of her mom's head to grip the *kotinos*, the sage green olive wreath that crowns each Paralympic champion.

• • •

Tanni was born in Cardiff, Wales, in 1969. After her mother delivered, doctors found a tiny lump on Tanni's back, a clue that the baby's spinal cord was tangled with her spine. Tanni was diagnosed with spina bifida, but that was all her parents were told.

"The hospital didn't explain what it was and what was going to happen to me," Tanni has said. "Nobody told me my walking was going to deteriorate and that I'd end up in a wheelchair."[2]

Significant progress has been made over the last fifty years, and today many doctors counsel new parents that babies diagnosed with spina bifida can go on to live full lives. In Tanni's case, since neither she nor her family knew what to expect, they adopted an attitude of acceptance — and got on with life.

Tanni's grandfather encouraged her ambition early on. He passed on to her his own philosophy, that in the face of any obstacle or defeat, you should practice resilience. His motto, which Tanni adopted, was "Aim high, even if you hit a cabbage."

"It's about having a goal and a dream," she says. "It's about challenging people around you. I took it in my sports world to mean that you've got to be on the start line, you train hard and you don't give up. Lots of young people are frightened of failure. I was lucky in sport that I failed a lot before I became any good.

"I'm not very good at people saying, 'you can't do that,' especially if it relates to me being disabled. If you tell disabled children the things they can't do, it's very easy to believe it. My grandfather's motto gave me a chance to ignore the people I wanted to ignore and do the things I wanted to do. I also had a huge amount of parental support around me to make that happen."

• • •

As a toddler, Tanni could walk and run around with her older sister, and it wasn't until she turned five or six that the paralysis started to set in. The process was slow, with her legs unable to support her growing body. At a charity walk with friends, when walking was becoming more difficult, reality began to sink in. "It was one of those occasions when I realized other people didn't think I was normal," says Tanni. She walked as part of a large group and was puzzled when the crowd began to applaud her.

Later, the local paper wrote a story about her. "I felt that was wrong," Tanni has said. "I've never been comfortable with the 'poor born cripple' reports, and didn't see why I should be the centre of attention."[3]

Tanni's parents were always keen on her becoming self-reliant, being very conscious that when they died, Tanni would need to be able to take care of herself. Their marriage was a balanced partnership, an example of equality, and they were both foundational to Tanni's independence.

"When I was about seven, my dad, who was an architect, showed me a book," says Tanni. "It had pictures of the Taj Mahal and Sydney Opera House, and all of these amazing buildings. He told me I need to get a good job so I can travel around the world. That was a life-changing moment for me. I've now been to pretty much every building that was in that book."

Tanni's mother was a strong feminist, a woman who always had her own money to spend. She, too, pushed Tanni to gain autonomy from a young age, encouraging her to go to a weeklong horse-riding camp away from home when Tanni was just nine years old.

By the time she turned twelve, it was clear that Tanni would use a wheelchair, and that was a positive experience:

her wheelchair increased her mobility, giving her a new level of independence. Suddenly she could once again do those things her legs wouldn't support any longer: run away from her mother, chase after her older sister, and spend time with her friends.

She has said, "Some people might find [it] hard to understand, but the trouble is there is this perception that walking is good and not walking is bad. For me that's not true because being in a wheelchair has given me more mobility not less."[4]

Navigating school in a wheelchair was initially a positive experience, due in large part to the wonderful support she got from her junior school's headmaster, Dewi Thomas. But by the time she was a teenager, it became a challenge when the local secondary school refused to admit her, claiming it was because the school was inaccessible. Tanni had never been treated differently up to that point, and it was the beginning of her understanding the challenges of living with a disability.

"It didn't make any sense to me," she has said. As far as Tanni knew, there was only one difference between her and other children. "I knew I was sitting at a different height from other people, but that was as far as it went."

• • •

Tanni doesn't remember a time when she wasn't involved with sport. After an intense surgery that left her in a full body cast for six months, she could no longer ride horses, so she began trying out new sports. Her teachers and friends all encouraged her as she participated alongside her nondisabled peers — swimming, playing basketball, and rock climbing.

At a sports day at a school for children with disability, thirteen-year-old Tanni tried wheelchair racing for the first time and won a medal in the 60 meter event. Shortly after, in 1981, Tanni was selected to represent Wales at the Junior National Games. There she not only won a silver medal in the 100 meter race, but also set a British record when she took home a gold in slalom.[5]

After that, Tanni was hooked — and she returned to Nationals every year, right as attention for wheelchair racing started to take hold in the UK. She was inspired by Chris Hallam, the "bad boy of wheelchair racing," as she has described him, who lived very near to her. Watching him in the London Marathon in 1984, she thought to herself, "I could do that."

Tanni went on to enroll in Loughborough University, where she studied politics and social administration. It was there, in 1987, that she got her first racing chair, bought for her by the Cardiff branch of the Rotary Club. With the Paralympics approaching the following year, in Seoul, South Korea, she started to focus on strength training and increasing her mileage. Tanni had no idea how qualifications worked, but her goal was to become as fit and fast as possible.[6] She had a wingspan of five feet, ten inches, could bench press one-and-a-half times her own body weight, and logged at least seven miles a day. She trained on a loop around campus and started to enter more local road races.

The following summer, in 1988, Tanni was home from university when a letter arrived. A wheelchair emblem marked the front of the brown envelope. She ripped it open, knowing what it said. The letter invited Tanni to compete with the British Paralympic Team in Seoul — her first Paralympic Games.

Upon arriving in Seoul, Tanni didn't feel too much pressure since it was her first Games. Still, she was devastated when she came in fourth at her first event, the 100 meter race, and trailed in her second event, the 200 meter event. But she prevailed in her final event, the 400 meter race, winning the bronze medal and a place on the podium.

Her time in that race was eighty-one seconds, a new British record. She has said, "It was a big moment . . . I got back to the [athlete's] village and rang home as soon as I could . . . It was the middle of the night in Cardiff and I think Mum was more excited than I was."[7]

Tanni's experience in Seoul was the catalyst for her sporting career. In the nineteen years that followed, she went on to compete at four more Paralympic Games and subsequently became one of Britain's greatest para athletes of all time — winning sixteen Paralympic medals, thirteen World Championship medals, and six London Marathons and holding over thirty world records.

When Tanni decided to retire from sport in 2007, she did so very deliberately by picking her final competition on home turf: the 2007 Paralympic World Cup in Manchester, UK, where she took home the silver medal in the 200 meter race.

Just three years later, Tanni would find her next calling — serving the UK in the House of Lords.

. . .

Over the course of Tanni's sporting career, she received an impressive number of honors besides the medals she won — and that list has grown even longer since she left the world of competitive sport. Tanni was appointed to the Order of the British Empire, first as a Member (MBE), then as an Officer (OBE), and most recently as a Dame Commander (DBE) in 2010. In the British order of chivalry, her formal title is Baroness Grey-Thompson, DBE. Additionally, she has received honorary degrees from many universities.

After retiring, Tanni found herself increasingly interested in politics, an arena she never imagined she'd enter when she was younger. But she found moving from sports to politics wasn't too difficult; in fact, she views them as quite similar. In both fields, she says, you spend a lot of time preparing and have a limited time to achieve things. And just like in sport, in politics there's always another opportunity, another vote, another chance to do things differently.

She still doesn't like party politics, so serving as a cross-bench peer in the House of Lords — an independent — suits her well.[8]

"I had the chance to start serving in the House of Lords at age forty, which is quite young," says Tanni. "A friend told me I'd be stupid to turn down this opportunity, both because it might not come up again, but also because it was a chance to change things. I decided it was worth giving it a go."

Tanni acknowledges there is much she'd like to change, including more respect for wheelchair accessible parking spaces. She'd also like to make trains throughout the UK more accessible, joking that she wants "the same miserable commute as everyone else." And in the field of sport, Tanni hopes to make programs more widely available for young disabled athletes.

"At the moment, in the UK, a person with a physical disability is either a Paralympian or nothing," says Tanni. "It's really hard. There are loads of disabled kids who aren't very good at sport, but they would like to participate. We need to make it easier for disabled children to be active. Too often we either make excuses or make programs exclusive to nondisabled children.

"There are plenty of benefits [from physical activity] related to health and mental well-being. It was expected that

I would get loads of urinary tract infections as a child, but I didn't, because I was active. To me it's about getting people thinking about the benefits, rather than the barriers."

After Tanni stopped competing, she volunteered with Wheelchair Racing Association events. She acknowledges that it's still difficult for children with a disability, since many mainstream schools and physical education teachers don't have specialist training in disability sport. But she laments the lack of independence she sees among young people today.

"I have found that a lot of disabled thirteen-year-olds have absolutely no independence at all," says Tanni. "They don't know how to brush their teeth or have a shower because somebody else has always done that for them. Some of that comes from home and some of it comes from school where they have not been encouraged to fend for themselves. They might come to a flight of steps and it would never occur to them to get out and pull their chairs up after them."

• • •

As Tanni reflects on all of her accomplishments, she says she hopes to be regarded for her athletic achievements just like any other nondisabled person would be. She doesn't think of her success as an example of overcoming adversity: she is simply an athlete who happens to have a disability.

"It's actually not about overcoming adversity," she says. "It's really about overcoming discrimination. It's the low-level discrimination that's the most difficult to deal with, like when someone books a meeting room that is inaccessible."

At times, people don't know how to react around disabled people and end up feeling embarrassed. Tanni's theory is that happens because disabled people have been segregated in society for so long. Nondisabled people are uncomfortable simply because they're not used to being around someone who is different from them. Her advice is simple: treat disabled people as you would anyone else.

"The UK did some research and found a lot of people have never spoken to a disabled person," says Tanni. "And many are quite scared of it. My parents taught me to deal with discrimination. I remember being in the supermarket and seeing people dragging their kids out of my way, saying 'don't get too close, you might catch it.' My mom would respond, 'It's not contagious, you know.'"

As a parent herself now, Tanni sees immense value in integration. Since Tanni's daughter, Carys, is an only child who grew up around a lot of disabled people, it's the norm for her.

"In childhood, she saw pretty much every kind of impairment. Carys is kind, caring, and sensitive. She recognizes if people need some support and knows the right things to say; it's just amazing," says Tanni, "which goes to show that more people should be around disabled people just to have a better understanding."

One of those other disabled people Carys grew up with is her father, Tanni's husband, Dr. Ian Thompson. He is also a wheelchair racer.

Tanni and Ian always knew they wanted children, but knew that others had different views. She says one doctor had the attitude that "we might breed, and we might spread," and offered to terminate her pregnancy.

Tanni encountered "pregnancy prejudice" in public, too, with countless people fascinated by her fertility, sometimes asking rude or personal questions. But Tanni believes that people aren't deliberately impolite, which helps her avoid resentment and maintain a level head.

It's still a fact that fewer women with a disability have children, but that is changing. Medical advances are expanding the types of specialized pre- and postnatal care available, and social stigma is diminishing as more women with a physical disability do become mothers.

Carys is proof that Tanni doesn't let her spina bifida — or anything else — govern her life decisions and dreams. And that's what she hopes for other people with disabilities. She has said, recalling that motto learned early on, "if there was one thing that I could change, then it would be for young disabled people to naturally assume that they have a right to do everything their nondisabled counterparts are doing."[9]

Aim high, even if you hit a cabbage.

JUSTIN GALLEGOS

The only limit we have is our mind

Justin is a student at the University of Oregon and a professional distance runner, sponsored by Nike. He has cerebral palsy.

A VIDEO SHOWS THE UNIVERSITY OF OREGON running club meet on a fall Saturday morning. It opens with Justin Gallegos running to the finish line.[1] Justin is wearing a red sweatband, a green Oregon club vest over a black long-sleeved running top, black shorts, and green running shoes. His quad and calf muscles are wrapped with Rocktape. After crossing the finish line, he walks over to a trail display stand and collapses over it with outstretched arms — exhausted. He takes a moment to catch his breath, then joins the other finishers to chat about the morning's run before they leave to continue with the rest of their day.

Runners and spectators are casually dotted around the finish line. Among them is John Truax, Insights Director at Nike. He has a folder in his hand. John steps forward to speak.

After a few introductory remarks, John announces that Nike is awarding a professional athlete contract to Justin Gallegos. He warmly hugs Justin and the crowd erupts in applause. Justin, visibly shocked by this news and overwhelmed with emotion, collapses to his knees.

A few minutes later, John hands Justin a phone with his mom and dad on FaceTime. Justin's parents, who had been informed of and reviewed the contract beforehand, have to do all the talking as Justin is too emotional to speak.

Justin Gallegos was born with cerebral palsy. It mostly affects his legs and speech. With John Truax's announcement, he had just become the first athlete with cerebral palsy to be awarded a professional contract by Nike.

The date is October 6, 2018 — World Cerebral Palsy Day.

Getting that Nike professional contract brought Justin, aged 21, to national attention.

...

Justin was born in Santa Clarita, southern California.

"I was born with cerebral palsy. I didn't walk until I was three. And I wasn't officially diagnosed until that age.

"I was in a walker and braces until first grade."

Describing his upbringing, Justin says, "I grew up with two very loving parents, and I have one younger sister. My parents tried to raise me just like any other kid.

"I had some physical challenges in elementary school. I was getting interested in walking so I fell quite frequently. I was in adaptive PE and special education. I took horseback riding therapy for many years from when I was six months to thirteen. In elementary school I did karate lessons two or three times a week for a few years. Also in elementary school they would take us out to the playground and have us run around the grass soccer field; I loved it.

"When I got to junior high, PE was my favorite subject; I loved football, I loved track and field. I loved Fridays where they had us run around the entire soccer field."

On his dad's suggestion and with the support and encouragement of his high school coach, Larry David, Justin started cross-country running. "At first I wanted to play football because I really liked it. I grew up watching football. Because of certain aspects of football, Dad and I agreed it wasn't the right fit for me. So I tried running with the cross-country team."

In the beginning, Justin dragged his feet and fell a lot, but he persevered and improved over time. "In the beginning running wasn't easy. I fell quite frequently. Running is a different movement. You have to learn how to lift your knees and I wasn't quite used to that, but I still really enjoyed it and stuck with it.

"My dad and I sat down and set some goals. My season goal for my first year at high school was to run 5000 meters (3.2 miles) in under thirty minutes. I went out and did that in the first race of the season.

"My goal the next year was to run a mile in under eight minutes. That goal for me was equivalent to the others running the distance in under five minutes. I did it that year, and not even on our track. I did it at a seaside invitational, right down by the beach.

"I ran cross-country and track and field for all four years at high school, and year by year I continued to see my times drop."

As a senior in high school, Justin's cross-country three-mile personal record was 23:58 and his one-mile personal record was 7:08.

In June of his senior year, Justin was state champion in 400 meters and runner-up in 200 meters in the Paralympic ambulatory division at the California State Track and Field Championships. He was voted by his high school teammates as most inspirational runner four years in a row.

Justin graduated from high school in 2016, looking forward to the next stage.

• • •

When it comes to choosing a university, for those interested in athletics, University of Oregon (U of O) in Eugene has an excellent reputation. Justin applied to and was accepted there, but the out-of-state tuition costs were prohibitively expensive for his family.

Brent, Justin's dad, explains in an interview that Larry, Justin's high school coach, reached out to John Truax at Nike saying, "There has to be a way for this kid to go to this dream school, with as much work and effort as he's put into track and cross-country, and academically as well to get accepted to the university." John Truax responded by rallying a group of people to fundraise to help Justin attend U of O. Brent adds with emotion in his voice: "We can never really thank [John] enough."[2]

Justin acknowledges that he wouldn't be at the U of O without the support of both his coach, Larry, and John Truax. He explains that's also how he first became involved with Nike. "I have a disability and Nike was starting a project in the running department, called FlyEase. It's an easy-on, easy-off mechanism for shoes: you can put your foot into the shoe and zip it up — there's no tying of shoelaces. I tried out the first-generation prototype and gave feedback to the FlyEase team and have been testing for them ever since."

Justin loved his time in college. "U of O was a dream come true. I'm so glad I got to go there." He joined the college running club and his running went from strength to strength, over time moving to running longer-distance events. His many achievements were recognized in *Runner's World* magazine, which listed him as one of its Heroes of Running for 2017. The next year, in April 2018, he crossed the finish line for his first half marathon at Eugene in just over two hours.

It was just a few months later when Nike awarded him his professional contract captured in that video. On Instagram, Justin wrote, "This was perhaps the most emotional moment in my seven years of running! Growing up with a disability, the thought of becoming a professional athlete is as I have said before like the thought of climbing Mt. Everest! It is definitely possible, but the odds are most definitely not in your favor! Hard work pays off! Hundreds of miles, blood, sweat, and tears have led me here along with a few permanent scars!"[3]

The world-renowned Kenyan runner, Eliud Kipchoge, one of Justin's heroes, sent congratulations via Twitter: "Congratulations Justin, you earned it!"[4]

In April 2019, Justin achieved his dream of completing a sub-two-hour half marathon when he crossed the finish line of the Eugene Half Marathon in a time of 1:56:36. And in October 2019, he completed his first full marathon in Chicago in a time of 4:49:30. The day before, Eliud Kipchoge broke the two-hour record at the Berlin Marathon, which seemed somewhat poetic to Justin. Though the two runners are in contact on social media, they have yet to meet; Justin hopes he gets the opportunity to someday. In an interview with *Runner's World* after the marathon, Justin explained that his mission aligns with Kipchoge's: "To prove and show we can all be limitless," adding, "The only limit we have is our mind."[5]

Justin's dad, Brent, joined him in running that inaugural marathon. It was the first for Brent, too, he himself being a former sprinter and pole vaulter. Brent's early encouragement to Justin to try running has never let up. Father and son still share goals and Excel spreadsheets with training details, and they talk at least every other day. Justin's current goals include running the Chicago Marathon in under 4:20 and to complete a 50 kilometer run.

For Justin, the practice of setting goals has been a constant. He's always looking forward to the next race, to the next accomplishment. It's what he first learned from his dad and now uses in all aspects of his life — not just sports. It's a point he emphasized in his address to thousands of young people at the BBYO International Convention[6] in February 2019, where he received a Stand-Up Award, presented to a person who represents values of leadership and commitment: "As you look up to others, it is important to find your life; find what drives you; keep setting goals for yourself."[7]

One goal that has eluded Justin is participating in the Paralympics. Unfortunately, his Paralympic class includes athletes who are less disabled than he is, and he isn't able to meet the qualification times. This is a well-recognized problem with the Paralympic qualification system: successful athletes with disabilities not having an appropriate class for their level of disability. An additional problem is there are no half or full marathon events in the Paralympics for his disability class.

• • •

Justin is currently a senior at the University of Oregon's School of Journalism and Communications, majoring in advertising. He says that his success in sports has subconsciously driven him to succeed in academics and plan for the future.

He would like to complete college, get a job, continue with professional running, and do more motivational speaking. He also hopes to write a book.

"I'd like to get hired straight out of college and make an impact at the company I join."

He has his heart set on a particular job, and says, "If I get it, it will really be the 'bow on top.' It will be a huge, proud moment." He adds, "If I graduate and get this job, I really feel I will have gotten to the top and proved a lot of people wrong."

He also wants to stay in Oregon. "Oregon is where I've developed bonds and relationships with friends and teammates. Oregon is where I got signed. My friends and I share that bond of running in Oregon. I love running for a long period of time in the hills. Running in Oregon means a lot to me. I love the scenic aspect of it. I think running in Oregon has greatly impacted my life."

Justin wears that impact — literally. His first tattoo is of one of his favorite running spots, as he has explained on Instagram: "I don't get to go every weekend, but when I do it's nothing short of breathtaking. The top of the mountain is my favorite spot at Mount Pisgah. It's an incredible view. I highly recommend visiting this place. Being a trail runner, Pisgah is an awesome place to go, perfect for long trail runs! This tattoo reminds me of all my incredible running adventures in Oregon and the ones yet to come."[8]

Already Justin has gained valuable experience in preparation for life after graduation. "I've been running with the University of Oregon running club, working with Nike both on the FlyEase program and as a professional athlete, and working on an ad campaign for Nike at the J school [journalism school]."

He has also been honing his public speaking with an eye to that goal of being on the motivational speakers' tour. Before COVID-19 restricted speaking engagements in 2020, he had presented at Nike events on several occasions, in addition to giving talks at FedEx, Connecting Point of Park Cities, and more.[9] The Cerebral Palsy Alliance Research Foundation

(CPARF) also invited him to be their 2019 STEPtember Ambassador.[10]

•••

Reflecting on his life so far, Justin has much to say about living with a disability.

His advice for the parent of a child with disability is straightforward: "Don't treat them differently and never give up. That's exactly how my family treated me." He appreciates that his own parents were not like the many naysayers he bumped up against when he was a young boy. "There were a lot of adults in my elementary school telling me what I could and couldn't do, saying things like 'you can't go play soccer with the other kids in the soccer field.' They were overprotective of my cerebral palsy, afraid I would get hurt."

Some kept at him right through to graduation, he says. "Some people in high school doubted my ability to handle college."

That's where Justin's success at running helped him, though. It made a difference on so many levels, including dealing with those doubters: "When I succeeded at running, I found that people changed their attitude toward me. Running is very important for me. Running is my safe space. I became somebody in running. I felt like one of the guys. Running empowered me as a person. People sometimes think just because you have a physical disability, you also have an intellectual disability. This is so wrong."[11]

He acknowledges the paradox of aiming high but still wanting to be included. "In high school, I set the bar higher for myself. I wanted to be 'different,' but in a way I wanted to be seen just like everyone else, as one of the guys. I am like everyone else: I do get stressed, I have anxiety."

He emphasizes the importance of encouraging others: "One push to a friend, family member, or colleague could change their life. Like my father suggested, I ran cross-country eight years ago, and that changed my life."[7] In fact, it became almost a metaphor for his life — for dealing with challenge: "I like the wild side of trail running. I like running through rocks and different terrains, because it's a challenge. I like it because so many people told me what I could and couldn't do. Trail running is one of the hardest sports out there — it's really why I'm drawn to it.

"I'm also really drawn to this idea of being your own person. You have the power to go the distance. You have the power to be your own boss and be your own success. I personally believe nothing stops you. Your worst enemy is yourself. People now let too many things from the outside world hold them back. My idea of being an entrepreneur isn't necessarily being an inventor. It's taking the power into your hands, saying, 'Hey, I'm going to make my way up. I'm going to do something and make something. I'm going to show people it's possible. I'm going to fail forward. I'm going to fall down and get back up.'"

He's displayed that attitude in his accomplishments. Besides completing the Chicago Marathon, some of his proudest moments have been working with Nike. "Everything I've had the opportunity to do with Nike has been incredible."

That's what he'd like to be remembered for, he says: "For the impact I have on sport, for the impact I have on Nike and the FlyEase project, for the impact I have on people. I would like to be remembered for my story, for showing — not just disabled people but everyone — that if you set your mind to something, it's possible."

He's quick to add that having a disability and being an inspiration do not go hand-in-hand: just because you have a disability, doesn't mean you're an inspiration. "I've met people with disability and they weren't very inspirational. What's important is how you deal with your disability — not letting your disability hold you back."

There's not much doubt that's exactly what Justin will be remembered for — judging by the response to the video of his emotional reaction on learning about his Nike sponsorship deal. It's gone viral, striking a chord with many, with about 600,000 views to date.

Justin Gallegos's story is one for the ages.

RACHEL WOBSCHALL

Seize the world

Rachel has had a long career in
government, education, and health.
She has spastic diplegia.

THE CORN BELT in midwestern United States has been an important agricultural region since the mid-nineteenth century. It covers a rough square of states, thirteen in number, from North Dakota down to Kansas, east across to Kentucky and north to Michigan. The area is characterized by level land and rich soil — it's very good farming land.

Minnesota lies on the northern border of the Corn Belt, where Rachel Wobschall was born early in Rochester, in the late 1950s.

"I was born six weeks early," explains Rachel, "which isn't that early by today's standards, but it was back then. My parents were super young — my mother was eighteen and my dad was twenty-two. I was their first child, born just shortly before their first wedding anniversary.

"When my mom went in to premature labor, my parents didn't have insurance at the hospital, so they had to leave and get money at the bank, to pay before being admitted."

Rachel later came to wonder about this, given her condition. Rachel has spastic diplegia, which primarily affects her walking and balance.

• • •

"When I was around two years old, for a variety of reasons my parents returned home to live in Waseca — the town where they had both grown up. There, my maternal grandparents owned a family restaurant. Situated about an hour and fifteen minutes from St. Paul [the state capital], Waseca is largely a farming town with a population of about six thousand people back then," Rachel says.

Rachel wasn't able to walk until she was about four years old. "In the early days I couldn't put my feet down flat. I then had heel cord lengthening surgery on both sides, and after that I started to walk."

Rachel was an only child until she was seven, when her younger brother Rick arrived. Her mom herself had been an only child, which meant Rachel got a lot of attention. She says, "I was the focal point of both my parents' and my maternal grandparents' lives — they were all very involved. There was also extended family locally. I got a lot of adult input."

Rachel's parents both worked at the restaurant, and Rachel and her brother also worked there during the summer. They grew up with a strong work ethic, she says. "My parents were adamant that we work there in the summer, but not during the school year so that we could focus on school. We learned hard work early in life. We also learned to be able to interact with people; for example, the regulars who would stop by for coffee in the morning. But at an early age we also learned to interact in situations that might have been considered more adult, given alcohol was served."

Working at the restaurant also gave Rachel a strong sense of her community.

Rachel's mom, Carol, was an early role model and someone she has remained close to throughout life. "My dad cared about me, but my mom was the one who took me to appointments and did all that. My mom didn't see me as someone with a disability. My mom's attitude was, 'I just knew we had work to do.'"

Her parents' marriage later broke up when Rachel graduated from college. Her dad is now deceased. Her mom and brother still live in Waseca.

• • •

Rachel's route through school was relatively smooth. She says, "I went to regular school from kindergarten right through to twelfth grade. I was able enough to function pretty well in everything. The only thing that was always a hassle was physical education — there really was no knowledge of adaptive physical education. Fortunately, they were just starting a women's swim team when I was in high school. I wasn't particularly good, but I joined."

What she was very good at was academics. "I studied. I got the message early on, 'Go to school, make something of your life.'" Education was a priority for Rachel's mom, Carol. While she always made clear to Rachel that she was thrilled to be a mother, she wanted Rachel to have an education first. "My mother always wanted to get a college education and ultimately did." (When she was around fifty, Carol completed her undergraduate degree and then a master's.)

Rachel was also very active in extracurricular opportunities. She says, with a smile, "I'm kind of verbal. At high school I was on the debate team, and I got to go to an elite debate camp. I was also really active in student council and became a member of the statewide student council."

Throughout these growing-up years, Rachel always had the strong support of both family and community: "I always felt that people there were interested in seeing me succeed. I had great support from teachers and people in the community.

The adage 'it takes a village to raise a child' was very true in my case."

As an example, she cites three really committed Girl Scout leaders. "They set a number of things that they wanted a group of us young girls to achieve. They fundraised to do things like take us to Washington, D.C." Many of these young Girl Scouts themselves went on to college, something that was less common at the time in Waseca.

Rachel graduated from high school in 1977 and considered a number of colleges, eventually settling on University of St. Thomas in St. Paul. Laughing, she admits that some of her friends from the statewide student council, who were headed to Harvard and Princeton, said to her, "Rachel, you're setting your sights too low." This encouragement, however, was countered by others who thought quite the opposite — that she should stay much more local than St. Paul.

Rachel admits that her main goal was to get to the Twin Cities (St. Paul and Minneapolis). "I was thrilled to be going to St. Thomas. For me, it was 'Get me out of here. I want to get out of these cornfields. I've got to see a bigger world!'"

• • •

The year that Rachel started at University of St. Thomas — a private Catholic university — was the year the university became coed.

"I was in the first coed class in a university that at that time had about five thousand men and one hundred women. Our small group of female students was vastly outnumbered by male students."

Rachel was also the first in her family to attend university. She is a person of many firsts.

At orientation, Rachel introduced herself to the dean and the president, walking up to them and shaking their hands. Soon everyone at St. Thomas would know Rachel Wobschall, as she immersed herself in college life.

She knew she wanted to be a political science major from the start. Her grandmother's dad had been a state legislator. Her grandmother, who was a big influence in Rachel's life, wasn't politically active, but she was politically aware. "She always read the news. She always commented on things. I think very early on a seed got planted that this was important work. And then as I got involved with student council in high school and increasingly in student government in college, I settled on a political science major."

Rachel says, "I absolutely loved college." And she realized that St. Thomas with its majority of male students was a very good fit for her: "The things I wanted to do in life were going to involve more men than women, and I wanted to be able to be on an equal footing with men."

She soon became deeply active in student politics — rising through various positions over the years to becoming the first female president of the university's student body. In her final year, she was the first female recipient of the Tommie Award (changed from the earlier Mr. Tommie Award). This award is presented annually to a college senior who, according to the college body — students, faculty, and staff — "through scholarship, leadership, and campus involvement, best represents the ideals of St. Thomas Aquinas."

Rachel graduated from St. Thomas with a bachelor's degree in 1981.

• • •

Rachel credits both serendipity and well-planned work experience during her college years for shaping her career.

"Shortly after I started my political science 101 class, Rudy Perpich, a fellow freshman and son of Governor Rudy Perpich, then governor of Minnesota, asked me, 'Are you that person who was involved in student council at high school?' And I said, 'Yeah.' And he said, 'Well, you're probably the person who wrote that paper my dad talks about — he told me to read it, because it was written by somebody my age, about what kids could do to make their schools accessible.'"

Rachel explains: "The governor had a sister-in-law with multiple sclerosis, and he built a very attractive ramp into the governor's residence, which was pretty radical at the time [the seventies]. It came up at our state student council convention. I had written a paper about accessibility and spoke about it at the convention. John Kingrey from the governor's office was present and asked me to send a copy of the paper, which I did, and I received a nice letter back from the governor's office which I filed in my scrapbook."

That was the serendipity; the work experience was her own planning: "During what's called J-term, a January term, or an interim period, I had already organized to work for Tim Penny who was a state senator from our area. So, I worked at the Capitol during J-term in my freshman and sophomore years."

· · ·

Soon after graduating, Rachel began working in government, continuing there for almost two decades, and rising to become a senior staff member, reporting to the governor's chief of staff.

Over the years, Rudy Perpich, who was a three-term governor, became both a mentor and role model.

"He was a really progressive individual and governor. He appointed a lot of women to very high-powered positions in the eighties. Under his leadership, I began to think that women could achieve anything."

One of her roles in government was supervising preparation of all appointments to the executive branch, judiciary branch, and public sector. Another was executive director of a program working on technology for people with disabilities. This led to the Technology-Related Assistance for Individuals with Disabilities Act of 1988, also known as the Tech Act, which became a model for federal legislation. In this work, Rachel was always careful to ask for and include the voice of people with disabilities and their families. She later helped with the rollout of legislation in other states.

As a further display of her strong work ethic, Rachel completed a master's in international management at St. Thomas during her time with government. She was then recruited to her alma mater to run its alumni program. While there, she completed a PhD in organizational development. With that achievement, she earned the accolade known as the "St. Thomas triple crown," for earning her three degrees from the university.

During her time at St. Thomas, she served on the board of directors at Gillette Children's Specialty Healthcare, where she herself later became an adult patient. After more than a decade at St. Thomas, Rachel went to work as Director of Principal Gifts at Gillette for over five years. In 2021, Rachel started a new role as Planned and Major Gift Officer at True Friends.

What does Rachel attribute her fulfilling and successful life
to? The answers are many and include:

- To, first and foremost, "the love and support of my
  family and friends. I have always known that there were
  many people in my corner, and I have always tried to
  pay forward their generosity."[1]
- To being, as she says, "a little fearless. In my family,
  there was nobody telling me 'no' — there was nobody
  telling me that I couldn't have ambition."
- To being "a lifelong learner both inside and outside the
  classroom."[1]
- To having many role models and mentors, starting
  with her mom. "Others included people I worked for
  over the years: the late Governor Rudy Perpich; Mark
  Dienhart, then at St. Thomas and the person who
  recruited me to work there; Steven Bosacker, chief of
  staff for former Governor Jesse Ventura."
- To having been able to develop routines that support a
  healthy lifestyle: "I normally swim, bike, and ski. I regularly work with a personal trainer, physical therapist,
  and massage therapist."
- To having many interests: "I maintain an active social
  life, and when I can, I travel both nationally and
  internationally."
- To having had few hiccups related to her disability
  thus far in life: "I had some back issues in my late
  twenties and early thirties which prompted me to discover Pilates and massage, which have largely erased
  the problems. I experienced some knee pain in my

mid-fifties. Traditional and specialized medical professionals were quick to say that it was a result of my CP (cerebral palsy); I needed to advocate for myself and not be satisfied that blaming my CP for acute issues would become a way of life for me. As it turned out, my knee pain was due to osteoarthritis. I underwent successful knee replacement surgery, which eliminated the knee pain. One point to note: the post-surgery rehabilitation took longer than would typically be expected for this type of surgery. I successfully regained the ability to walk after the surgery . . . I have been an independent walker my entire life, though in later years I have started using walking sticks outside the home, finding them more practical than crutches."[1]

• And finally, to living with spastic diplegia: "Living with this condition has helped me to develop a broader and bolder vision, creativity, and a willingness to persevere toward a desired outcome. I believe that my diagnosis is one aspect of my personhood that makes me fully human."[1]

. . .

As Rachel reflects on her life so far, what rises to top of mind is the overall treatment of cerebral palsy, what she has achieved in life and would still like to, the aging process, and advice she would give others.

"There hasn't really been any huge breakthrough in the treatment of cerebral palsy in the past twenty-five years," she says. She laments the fact that "families still have such a hard time even getting the basics, like good information, good resources." But she speaks enthusiastically about the 2019 international symposium, Improving Quality of Life for

Individuals with Cerebral Palsy through Treatment of Gait Impairment, that Dr. Novacheck at Gillette organized, with which she was involved. (The proceedings from the symposium were later published in book format.[2]) She also likes what organizations such as the CP Research Network are doing — a number of years ago, she contributed as part of a large community, setting a research agenda.

Rachel recognizes that she has had an opportunity to know many people with disabilities who haven't lived to be the age that she is now. That still drives her: "I'm still here, so there's more for me to do." She makes a deliberate effort to try to be as supportive as she can be to others because, as she says, "I was so fortunate to be the recipient of that." Nowadays she serves on boards to support people with various disabilities, adding that, "the needs don't go away."

Rachel advises people to follow their interests and passions. "There's a way through the door to do what you want to do. That's true for anybody, whether they have a disability or not. It's a struggle for all of us every day — don't use anything as an excuse. There are things we're good at and things that we're not, and it's okay to make choices, but don't let somebody else's opinion of you be your limiter."

She recalls times when well-meaning individuals wanted her to direct her efforts toward disability. While at university, a counselor suggested she abandon her degree in political science and change universities to become a vocational rehabilitation counselor herself. Rachel was having none of it. She admits, "It's hard for each of us to figure out what our life should be — don't let somebody else dictate what *your* life should be."

Rachel is finding the aging process interesting. She recalls many years ago, when she was working in government, a woman with disability told her that she had experienced more discrimination as an older woman than as a person with a disability. Noting how very youth-oriented American culture is, she says that both disability and age discrimination need to be addressed.

. . .

Eighteen-year-old Rachel Wobschall happily left behind the cornfields of Minnesota to live in St. Paul to pursue a fulfilling career and travel the world. But she has never forgotten her roots. Today, she enjoys frequent visits back to Waseca. For her family and community there, she holds both deep love and tremendous appreciation.

ELIZABETH KOLBE HARDCASTLE

Just keep swimming

Elizabeth (Beth) is a lawyer in Washington, D.C., and a retired Paralympic swimmer. She became paralyzed as a result of a car accident in adolescence.

DRIVING DOWN THE FREEWAY IN SEATTLE, with the tall, snowy peak of Mount Rainer in the background, sixteen-year-old Elizabeth Kolbe Hardcastle — known familiarly as Beth — looks out the window as a billboard catches her eye. The sign looming above the freeway shows a photo of a girl, a student much like Beth. In the picture, the student, Brooke Ellison, wears a black graduation cap and gown as she sits in her motorized wheelchair.

Brooke is beaming.

For Beth, that photo of Brooke displayed possibility. "I saw a billboard with a girl in a power chair and a Harvard graduation cap on," Beth later told a reporter. The caption was "Quadriplegia at Harvard: A+."[1]

"It does feel like such a pivotal moment in my life," says Beth of seeing the poster. "It was so fleeting. It was a quick look as we were driving, barely any time at all. And yet, it felt so impactful. It felt like the first time I realized what I could still do, and what could still be possible."

Beth had always been smart, excelling in school long before the car accident that rendered her paralyzed at age fourteen. Two years after she saw that billboard, she would go on to be high school valedictorian and apply to Harvard. But until that moment, she never thought attending an Ivy League university was even in the realm of possibility.

"In a weird way, it was the accident and that billboard that made me think, 'Oh, maybe I can go to Harvard.' It was incredibly meaningful," says Beth.

When Beth faces a challenge, it's maxims like the message on the billboard that keep her ambitions high. In her bedroom, a poster with the words "Just keep swimming" hangs on the wall, a gift from her sister. To Beth, it's another aphorism she lives by: keep going, keep working. And above all, don't have limits.

. . .

On a country lane in the flat expanse of rural Ohio, a nearly full moon illuminates the road ahead. Cindy Kolbe drives the car while her three passengers sleep quietly: her fourteen-year-old daughter, Beth, along with her fifteen-year-old daughter, Maria, and Maria's friend. After a two-hour journey, it's past midnight and they're almost there — just ten more minutes until they get home.

It's May 2000, and peaceful clouds hang across the night sky. As Cindy feels herself start to doze off, she rolls down the window. She feels the strong pull toward sleep and the heaviness of her eyelids closing. Suddenly, the car swerves and flattens a road sign. Screams erupt as the car veers into a ditch, rolls three times, and lands on its roof.

Silence follows.

Another driver who sees the accident calls for help, and shortly after, headlights appear as firefighters arrive at the scene. Cindy, Maria, and her friend get out of the overturned car independently. But Beth, in the front passenger seat, is trapped.

Cindy later wrote in her memoir of the moments after the accident:

Everything — the whole world — twists and mutates. The life we knew falls to pieces, irrevocably broken . . . Beth's legs disappear in a cave of wreckage. Fear paralyzes me. I don't know what to do. The fireman chats with her about school and volleyball . . . A Life Flight helicopter is on the way. Someone reassures me that it's simply a routine precaution. It's not. The Jaws of Life tears into metal with bursts of harsh light and piercing squeals.[2]

Beth is rushed into a helicopter, and Cindy and the other two girls are ushered into their own ambulances, their injuries less severe.

As Cindy reunites with her younger daughter at the hospital, she feels another heavy wave of regret and responsibility when she learns the extent of Beth's injury. Doctors advise that the bones in Beth's neck shattered and cut her spinal cord.

. . .

Amazingly, from the very moment Beth learned she had become a quadriplegic — paralyzed below the waist with limited movement through her arms — she adopted a hopeful spirit. She has said of that time, "The most defining — and, in many ways, positive — moment of my life might also be considered the most tragic by those who do not know me."[3]

That optimism carried Beth through the months that followed her injury, as she endured countless hours of treatment and therapy. During rehab, Beth attended a wheelchair clinic to be measured for her own chair. At her appointment, she was offered a choice: either a motorized wheelchair that would give her maximum mobility and speed, but required use of a specialized car, or a manual chair, which could fit inside any car.

Beth answered the question of which to choose with another question: "Will I get stronger faster using only a manual chair?"[4]

She says, "Sometimes I look back and I wonder how I was able to do all of that. Being fourteen and having the support of friends and family like I did, I just didn't know any better, to question or to think differently.

"I'm a naturally positive person. I think that certainly helped. I think being young also makes you more resilient. I wasn't set in my ways and didn't have to grapple with reidentifying myself at that time in life."

It also helped that Beth's medical team didn't weigh her down with predictions of limitations. No one said to her, "You're going to be in a hospital for the rest of your life" or "You'll need care twenty-four hours a day." That gave Beth a unique freedom — she never thought something was impossible, and she had the ability to define for herself what she could and couldn't do.

"I remember the physical therapist coming in and saying, 'Let's talk about all the things you can do like choir and sports and getting married,'" says Beth. "My mom was quite upset, asking, 'How can you tell this girl in intensive care that she can still do all these things? We don't know yet.' But to me, no one had told me I couldn't yet, so I believed it."

During her recovery, Beth relied heavily on Cindy's help, for everything from getting out of bed to driving to physical therapy appointments. Beth's dad, John, a teacher, also became her advocate. And it helped that Beth is the youngest child of the family. Her older brother, Ben, was already in college and away from home when she was a teenager. Maria, her sister, was still in high school, and while Beth's injury took attention away from her, she was incredibly supportive.

"My accident affected the whole family," says Beth. "When the focus converged on me, it was to the detriment of my mom, because she didn't get the help she needed early on for her depression."

At the time of her injury, Beth had no idea how deeply the accident had affected her mom's mental health. Cindy was plagued with headaches and fell into a deep fog for many years. She ultimately got help, but it wasn't until Beth was an adult that she realized the extent of her mom's hardships.

In the midst of her own struggles, Cindy's resolve was astounding. She maintained a total dedication to Beth — the kind of compassion and focus a mom can uniquely give their child. Beth felt that unconditional love from both of her parents.

"My parents are amazing. I love them," says Beth. "They were incredibly supportive from day one. They always believed in me and let me take the lead. So, when I wanted to apply for Harvard, they encouraged it, but they didn't push it. And the same is true for swimming."

· · ·

What began as physical therapy — a way to rebuild strength after her accident — soon developed into much more. Swimming became Beth's source of personal strength and an expression of her potential.

Just six months after she began training, Beth convinced her mom to drive her across state lines to the Michigan Wheelchair Games. Neither of her parents ever complained about the sacrifices they made to support her athletic pursuits, driving long hours and spending many weekends away from home at club meets.

In Michigan, Beth met Cheryl Angelelli, a Paralympic swimmer who went on to become a wheelchair dancer. Her husband was also a Paralympic coach. Together, they took Beth aside after watching her swim, and told her, "Beth, you could be really good. Why don't you go to Nationals and see what happens?"

Beth picked up the training pace and started swimming with local clubs near her home in Ohio. Her coaches learned how to adapt training programs to her abilities. Many of them, including Peggy Ewald, had never trained a swimmer with a disability.

"Peggy is the best," says Beth. "She didn't have a background in how to adapt my workouts. Peggy never had the mindset that 'Oh well, people with disabilities can only get this far. They can only swim this fast.' She took what she knew from being a swim coach of able-bodied athletes and experimented with me.

"When we tried to do flip turns, she got in the water with me, and it was so fun. It didn't work, but it was a good workout. A lot of her other efforts were successful, obviously."

Together, Peggy and Beth set down a path that would lead them both to the Paralympics. Over the next three years, Beth began traveling to club meets and competing at an elite level. During her senior year of high school, she participated at Paralympic Nationals and qualified for the Athens 2004 Paralympic Games. The steep upward slope of her athletic career was, amazingly, matched by the pace of her academic success: that same year, as a senior, Beth was named valedictorian and admitted to Harvard.

But that presented her with a tough choice: the Paralympics took place in mid-September, overlapping with the start of her first term at Harvard. Beth tried to find a way to do both, but she was nervous about moving to Cambridge, Massachusetts, and missing out on the first few crucial weeks of her first semester. It was a tough decision, but she opted not to compete in Athens, feeling confident that she would have another opportunity. Luckily, Beth's instinct was right.

When Beth began her freshman year, far from her home in Ohio, Cindy made an incredible sacrifice and moved to Massachusetts too. Both mother and daughter felt it was necessary to have an additional year together to make sure Beth could do it on her own.

"We had been attached at the hip for so long," says Beth. "Getting injured at fourteen was in some ways great because I was already at home and my mom was able to help me. By the time I left for college, I could take care of myself, and I was prepared to be independent. But I think we needed a buffer, just to make sure that was the case. I have fond memories of meeting my mom in Harvard Square and having lunch together."

With her mom's support, Beth began to thrive at Harvard. She quickly found her tribe, joining the Harvard swim team, first as a freshman team manager, and then as a full member of the varsity team. She traveled to international competitions, earning medals at several Paralympic World Cups and the Parapan American Games in Rio de Janeiro in 2007. The following year, Beth again qualified for the Paralympic team. This time, she accepted the invitation, and was named to Team USA for the Beijing 2008 Paralympic Games. Months after she graduated from Harvard with a bachelor of arts in health care policy, Beth made the trip to China.

"The Games experience was incredible, especially on the scale like it was in China," says Beth. "The opening ceremonies were massive. I wheeled in with the rest of the athletes; first, under the stadium and then out onto the floor of the Bird's Nest. It was completely packed. Nothing compares to the Bird's Nest [stadium]: massive crowds, massive cheering, and a beautiful display. China did a fantastic job putting together those opening ceremonies.

"I have strong memories of the ready room with my coach, getting amped up and excited. And of course, I remember the races, especially when I hit the wall in the 50 meter freestyle. I remember looking back and seeing that I made fifth place. I thought I was probably going to come in seventh, so it was great. It was incredibly meaningful."

Beth left Beijing after two successful races — besides placing fifth in the 50 meter freestyle, she came in eighth in the 50 meter backstroke. That fall, she already had her eyes set on her next chapter: applying to Stanford Law School and pursuing a career in policy.

• • •

"The first time I realized that I wanted to do law school was when I took an advanced placement course in government in high school," says Beth. "I loved that class so much. That year, I also went to Washington, D.C., for a weeklong program with the National Youth Leadership Network. D.C. is full of great advocates, and I fell in love with the city."

Beth's time in Washington left a strong impression on her. So strong, that while at Harvard, Beth returned to spend a summer interning in Senator John Kerry's office, where she led policy work on stem cell research and even joined Kerry on the Senate floor for the 2006 stem cell debate.

"It was a dream come true," says Beth. "John Kerry is an incredible man. I'm a huge fan. That summer, everyone was focused on health care issues and the stem cell debate. It was an incredible opportunity. It solidified that I wanted to go to law school."

At Stanford, Beth once again thrived. She served as president of the National Association of Law Students with Disabilities, and while she enjoyed working on disability rights, she opted instead to pursue a career in health care policy.

"There's definitely an expectation that if you have a disability and go to law school, you're going to work on disability rights," says Beth. "One of my mentors, Andy Imparato, is the head of the Disability Rights Center. He said we need more people with disabilities in the legal profession who are *not* doing disability rights, who can change the industry from the inside.

"I loved that. I care deeply about disability rights, and I will always do my pro bono work in that area, but I want to expand access. I love that I can infiltrate the rest of the legal profession and recruit people with disabilities."

After graduation, when Beth interviewed with law firms, she had her sights firmly set on Washington, D.C. She remembers a job interview where the hiring team asked a series of inappropriate questions, like "How can you type?" In the moment, she didn't push back. Instead, she shut down and left as soon as she could, recognizing that it wasn't the law firm for her. She feels grateful that those experiences with discrimination are few and far between.

"As a white woman who went to good schools, I have a lot of privilege. I feel weird saying that I haven't experienced discrimination that much, because I know it is pervasive for people with disabilities. But I've been very lucky to not have had a lot of barriers because of my disability," says Beth. "When it does happen, it's helpful knowing it's just a small group of a people that will make you feel small. I think most people are good."

Beth has found that often discrimination occurs when people don't understand the person or don't have experience with a certain type of condition. That's why today, at her law firm Sidley Austin LLP, she is proud to be working on diversity in hiring.

"One of the things that is so wonderful about Sidley is that the firm has elevated me and made me a spokesperson, reflecting their interest in hiring a diverse set of lawyers," says Beth. "It's given me an opportunity to recruit students and attorneys with disabilities."

Beth works on policies that make health care more accessible for Americans, including issues related to drug prices and improving Medicare coverage of products, including wheelchairs. She notes that it's important to promote more people with disabilities into positions of power in health care. "Everyone with a disability has a story of a doctor who dismissed them or didn't give them the treatment they needed because they didn't see them as a full person; they just saw them as someone with a disability. And so they didn't get the care they needed.

"The more we can elevate diverse people and people with disabilities into positions of visibility and power, the better it will be."

* * *

Beth watched her friends begin to date in her teenage and college years, but she herself was a late bloomer. For many reasons, she didn't enter the dating scene until law school. Certainly she was highly focused on swimming before then, but her disability played a role as well. In high school, she just didn't feel comfortable about dating, and even in college, despite being interested in boys, she never made a move — afraid there may be a stigma related to dating a person with a disability.

She eventually learned that the bias was self-imposed. After she settled into her new home in Washington, D.C., Beth joined the dating app Hinge. She was still hesitant, afraid that people would see her in a wheelchair and automatically "swipe left," so she was pleasantly surprised when she connected with a number of interested suitors, including her future husband, Dan.

"I was shocked at how many responses I got," says Beth. "I met Dan on Hinge and had a wonderful first date. He didn't have a lot of experience with disability. But it was a nonissue to him. After a few months, I pushed him, and asked, 'How did it not bother you? Was it something you felt like you had to overcome?' And he said, 'No, I liked your pictures, and your bio was impressive. I just enjoyed talking to you.' So it wasn't something he felt like he had to overcome. It was so lovely."

Dan is a fellow lawyer, with a decade of experience developing progressive housing policy and working for democratic presidential campaigns. In May 2019, Beth and Dan married in Washington, D.C., and their wedding was featured in both *The Washingtonian* and *The New York Times*.

That same year, Beth's mom published her memoir, *Struggling with Serendipity*. For Cindy, writing was a helpful way to heal from the accident. The book brought Beth and

Cindy even closer, and helped Beth realize how her parents had experienced the accident and her disability.

"My mom has always been a great writer and for her, writing our story was really cathartic," says Beth. "Even though it was our story, the book included things that I wasn't aware of. I loved learning about my mom's perspective, but some of it was hard, because she hadn't been as open about her depression. I've become so proud of the work she's doing now and her advocacy, helping other moms of newly injured people with disabilities."

Like the billboard Beth saw when she was in Seattle, Cindy's book is a display of what is possible in life.

"My parents knew I would have challenges and they wanted to see what was possible," says Beth. "They let me forge my own path, because there wasn't a guidebook. We didn't really know how to do this. We didn't have a lot of resources or examples to look to, besides the billboard."

Beth's own journey could now be a billboard for others — offering hope and showing the power of possibility.

ACKNOWLEDGMENTS

First and foremost, thank you to each of you who participated in this book. We are greatly honored that you trusted us with your stories. We came from different backgrounds to write this book: Lily as the parent of a son with cerebral palsy and author of a book on the subject, and Kara as someone who works with many para athletes. Talking with you and writing your stories has had a profound effect on both of us.

Thank you to Micah Niermann, Barbara Joers, Tom Novacheck, Paula Montgomery, Timothy Feyma, and Andrea Stoesz at Gillette Children's Healthcare Press, our publisher. Thank you to our great production team: Carra Simpson (project manager), Ruth Wilson (editor), Olwyn Roche (illustrator), Jazmin Welch (cover artist and book designer), Lina Abdennabi, Greta Cunningham, and Rose Sullivan (marketing), and Megan Swartz Gellert (publicist). And thank you to Bright Wing Media for ebook production and Central Oregon Recording for audiobook production.

Our early readers were very important. We're grateful to them all for providing such useful feedback on various drafts. They include Ger Dundon, Máire Buckley, Nicolette Linse, Tommy Collison, Sandie McCanny, Carmel Murray, Clodagh Coman, Christine Simpson, Darragh Buckley, Lindsey Talley, Denis Collison, Edel Davin-Power, Sally-Shannon Birkel, Jeanine Amacher, Marusia Musacchio, Una Dunne-Shannon,

Sheena Pakanati, Kirstie Tiscareno, Christina Cacioppo, and Eimear O'Donnell.

Thank you also to Sylmara Multini and Mariana Magalhaes De Paula for their help with Portuguese translation for Daniel Dias.

Thank you to all those who took the time to read the book and write a review.

From Lily

Thank you to my husband Denis for everything — both in the writing of this book, but also in whole adventure of our life together. Thank you to Patrick, John, and Tommy, and their partners, Silvana, Laura, and Lindsey. I very much appreciate your interest and support in all my endeavors.

From Kara

Thank you to my husband Darragh for his endless support, encouragement, and love — I could not have done this without you. And to our son Solian and daughter Sage, who daily light up our lives. Thank you to my parents, Nicolette and Brian, for their essential help with childcare as I wrote.

APPENDIX 1

Physical Disabilities: Resources

If you are interested in learning more about physical disabilities included in this book, and inclusion of people with disabilities, the following resources will be of interest.

Blindness and vision loss
https://www.nhs.uk/conditions/vision-loss/

Cerebral palsy
https://www.gillettechildrens.org/conditions-care/cerebral-palsy/what-is-cerebral-palsy

Chapter 1 of Collison, L. (2020). *Spastic Diplegia—Bilateral Cerebral Palsy*. Gillette Children's Press. Available online: https://gillette childrenshealthcarepress.org/assets/images/books/documents/Spastic_Diplegia%E2%80%93Bilateral_Cerebral_Palsy-sample.pdf

Fibular hemimelia
https://www.stepsworldwide.org/conditions/fibular-hemimelia/

Malformations of arms and/or legs
https://www.cdc.gov/ncbddd/birthdefects/ul-limbreductiondefects.html

Muscular dystrophy
https://www.cdc.gov/ncbddd/musculardystrophy/index.html

Polio
https://www.nhs.uk/conditions/polio/

Restricted growth, also known as dwarfism and achondroplasia
https://www.nhs.uk/conditions/restricted-growth/symptoms/

Spina bifida
https://www.gillettechildrens.org/conditions-care/spina-bifida/what-is-spina-bifida

Spinal cord injury
https://www.gillettechildrens.org/conditions-care/spinal-cord-injury

Other conditions
https://www.gillettechildrens.org/conditions-care

Inclusion of people with disabilities:
www.cdc.gov/ncbddd/disabilityandhealth/disability-strategies.html

Information on:
- U.S. policy and legislation
- Universal design
- Accessibility
- Reasonable accommodations
- Assistive technology
- Independent living
- Assisted living
- Communicating with and about people with disabilities

APPENDIX 2

Information on Para Sport

If you are interested in learning more about Para sport, the International Paralympic Committee website has a lot of useful information: https://www.paralympic.org. The following web pages are of particular interest.

Explanatory Guide to Paralympic Classification: Paralympic Summer Sports June 2020
https://www.paralympic.org/sites/default/files/2020-10/2020_ 06%20Explanatory%20Guide%20to%20Classification_Summer%20 Sports.pdf

This guide includes an explanation of the classification system used for athletes competing in the Paralympics:

> Classification provides a structure for competition. Athletes competing in Para sports have an impairment that leads to a competitive disadvantage. Consequently, a system has been put in place to minimise the impact of impairments on sport performance and to ensure the success of an athlete is determined by skill, fitness, power, endurance, tactical ability and mental focus. This system is called classification. Classification determines who is eligible to compete in a Para sport and it groups the eligible athletes in sport classes according to their activity limitation in a certain sport.

> Ten eligible impairments are included, such as impaired muscle power and vision impairment.

This guide covers the following summer sports:

- Archery
- Athletics (includes track and field and wheelchair racing)
- Badminton
- Boccia
- Canoe
- Cycling
- Equestrian
- Football five-a-side
- Goalball
- Judo
- Powerlifting
- Rowing
- Shooting
- Sitting volleyball
- Swimming
- Table tennis
- Taekwondo
- Triathlon
- Wheelchair basketball
- Wheelchair fencing
- Wheelchair rugby
- Wheelchair tennis

Explanatory Guide to Paralympic Classification:
Paralympic Winter Sports July 2020
https://www.paralympic.org/sites/default/files/2020-10/2020_10%
20Explanatory%20Guide%20to%20Classification_Winter%20
Sports.pdf

In addition to the information on classification, this guide covers the following winter sports:

- Para alpine skiing
- Para ice hockey
- Para nordic skiing

- Para snowboard
- Wheelchair curling

International Paralympic Committee:
Classification by Sports
https://www.paralympic.org/classification-by-sport

This web page contains further information on individual sports.

ENDNOTES

Preface

1. Van der Slot, W.M., Nieuwenhuijsen, C., van den Berg-Emons, R.J., et al. (2010). Participation and health-related quality of life in adults with spastic bilateral cerebral palsy and the role of self-efficacy. *J Rehabil Med* 42(6): 528–535.
2. https://www.cp-achieve.org.au/
3. https://www.usatoday.com/story/sports/olympics/2016/09/09/brazils -daniel-dias-the-michael-phelps-of-the-paralympics/90123356/

Introduction

1. See Banks, J., Maître, B., McCoy, S., & Watson, D. (2016). Parental Educational Expectations of Children with Disabilities, https:// www.esri.ie/system/files/media/file-uploads/2016-05/RS50.pdf, and Organisation for Economic Co-operation and Development (2005) Students with Disabilities, Learning Difficulties and Disadvantages, Statistics and Indicators, OECD.
2. https://www.who.int/publications/i/item/9789241564182
3. Graham, H.K., Rosenbaum, P., Paneth, N., et al. (2016). Cerebral palsy. *Nat Rev Dis Primers* 2: 1–24.
4. See Kinsella, E., Richie, T., & Igou, E. (2017). Attributes and applications of heroes: A brief history of lay and academic perspectives. In S. Allison, G. Goethals, & R. Kramer (Eds), *Handbook of heroism and heroic leadership.* Routledge, 19–25, and Kinsella, E., Richie, T., & Igou, E. (2015). Lay perspectives on the social and psychological functions of heroes. *Front psychol* 6(130).

Lex Gillette

1. Adapted from Gillette, L. (2020). *Fly.* Unite Publishing.
2. https://aira.io/how-it-works

Jan Brunstrom-Hernandez

1. Brunstrom-Hernandez, J. (2015). *Meant to Live.* https://vimeo.com/142187305

Daniel Dias

1. https://danieldias.esp.br/daniel-dias/
2. https://www.usatoday.com/story/sports/olympics/2016/09/09/brazils-daniel-dias-the-michael-phelps-of-the-paralympics/90123356/

Judy Heumann

1. Heumann, J., & Joiner K. (2020). *Being Heumann: An Unrepentant Memoir of a Disability Rights Activist.* Beacon Press, 10.
2. *Being Heumann*, 27.
3. *Being Heumann*, 42.
4. *Being Heumann*, 57.
5. https://www.fordfoundation.org/media/4276/judyheumann_report_2019_final.pdf
6. *Being Heumann*, 3.

Jessica Long

1. Adapted from Long, J. (2018). *Unsinkable.* HMH Books.
2. *Unsinkable*, 27.
3. Olympians and Paralympians were previously required to be amateur athletes and were not permitted to receive compensation or enter into sponsorship agreements. In 1978, the Ted Stevens Olympic and Amateur Sports Act gave Olympic athletes the right to earn money through sponsorship or direct payment.
4. Wharton, D. (2018, September 21). U.S. Olympic leaders vote to give equal pay to Paralympic athletes. *Los Angeles Times.* https://www.latimes.com/sports/olympics/la-sp-usoc-paralympics-20180921-story.html
5. Penny, B. (2019, December 13). U.S. Olympic Committee significantly increases payments to athletes for Olympic/Paralympic, world medals, Team USA. https://www.teamusa.org/News/2016/December/13/US-Olympic-Committee-Significantly-Increases-Payments-To-Athletes-For-Olympic-World-Medals
6. https://www.paralympic.org/classification

7. https://www.paralympic.org/swimming/classification
8. https://www.paralympic.org/ailbhe-kelly
9. OlympicTalk (2021, February 7). Jessica Long, swimmer in 2021 Super Bowl commercial, has incredible personal story. NBC Sports. https://olympics.nbcsports.com/2021/02/07/jessica-long-super-bowl-commercial-swimmer-paralympics/

Ila Eckhoff

1. Newsday https://www.newsday.com/sports/high-school/high-school-athletes-thank-their-moms-on-mother-s-day-1.7985486
2. New York City Mayor's Office for People with Disabilities. (2016). *NYC at work–Ila Eckhoff* [Video]. https://www.facebook.com/watch/?v=1466732466688483
3. Eckoff, I. (2017). OptionB.Org. https://optionb.org/stories/grateful-sklz1l6px
4. Ecknoff, I. (2019, October 25). Employment matters for New Yorkers with disabilities: the right talent, right now. *Oswego County News Now.* http://www.oswegocountynewsnow.com/opinion/employment-matters-for-new-yorkers-with-disabilities-the-right-talent-right-now/article_7031181a-f66d-11e9-aa32-f7cb2b90a84e.html
5. Ila sits on the board of directors of both the Cerebral Palsy Foundation and RespectAbility.
6. RespectAbility. (2019). [Video]. https://www.respectability.org/2019/09/success-stories-of-self-advocates-being-real-with-yourself-and-advocating-for-yourself-unapologetically/

Chantal Petitclerc

1. https://sencanada.ca/en/content/sen/chamber/432/debates/028db_2021-02-16-e#55
2. Bryden, J. (2021, February 16). *Petitclerc recounts her own experience with disability in final MAID bill debate.* CBC. https://www.cbc.ca/news/politics/senate-final-debate-maid-bill-1.5916429
3. Felicien had an outstanding season and was one of Canada's top medal hopes, but in the 100 meter final she had a fall at the first hurdle and did not complete the race.
4. Even though Chantal turned down the award, Athletics Canada awarded it to her anyway. https://www.cbc.ca/sports/petitclerc-refuses-athletics-canada-award-1.505987

5. CBC News. (2016, March 19). [YouTube]. https://www.youtube.com/watch?v=OCilwSoO8ww

6. Petitclerc, C. (2017, November 3). A love letter to Canada. *West Jet Magazine.* https://www.westjetmagazine.com/story/article/love-letter-canada-senator-chantal-petitclerc

Jerron Herman

1. Great Big Story (2017, May 3). [YouTube]. Dancing Professionally With Cerebral Palsy. https://www.youtube.com/watch?v=lRMpE6gxf1o&feature=emb_logo

2. Burke, S. (2015, April 17). Review: Heidi Latsky Dance at Montclair State University. *The New York Times.* https://www.nytimes.com/2015/04/18/arts/dance/review-heidi-latsky-dance-at-montclair-state-university.html?searchResultPosition=1

3. Dance.com (2017, April 3). [YouTube]. Dancing Through Disability: How A Dancer With Cerebral Palsy Made His Dream A Reality 2017. https://www.youtube.com/watch?v=WbA_XYPZAPA&feature=emb_title

4. GBH News (2016, July 7). [Video]. 'On Display': Dancing With Cerebral Palsy. https://www.wgbh.org/news/2016/07/07/arts/display-dancing-cerebral-palsy

5. Jerron, H. (2019, January 10). Dance as art and therapy in cerebral palsy. *Developmental medicine and child neurology.* https://pubmed.ncbi.nlm.nih.gov/30632135/

6. https://www.tkc.edu/stories/2017-alumni-awards/

7. https://jerronherman.com

Ellie Cole

1. https://www.paralympic.org/feature/ellie-cole-s-out-body-experience-watching-rising-phoenix

2. Bonhôte, I., & Ettedgui, P. (Directors). (2020). *Rising Phoenix.* Netflix.

3. *Women's Health.* (2017, December 28). The Secret Life of Ellie Cole. https://www.womenshealth.com.au/the-secret-life-of-ellie-cole

4. "Butterfly effect" refers to a sensitive dependence on initial conditions, where a small change leads to large differences at a later state.

5. de Hosson, R. (2020, April 1). How Groundbreaking Tech Made Ellie Cole's Dream Come True. *Women's Health.* https://www.womenshealth.com.au/ellie-cole-tokyo-dream-paralympics

6. https://thewomensgame.com/news/ellie-cole-were-no-different-490
508

Jim Abbott

1. Abbott, J. & Brown, T. (2012). *Imperfect: An Improbable Life*. Ballantine
Books, 261–2.
2. *Imperfect*, 262.
3. *Imperfect*, 64–5.
4. *Imperfect*, 92.

Tom Shakespeare

1. https://farmerofthoughts.co.uk/collected_pieces/dating-dilemmas/
2. farmerofthoughts.co.uk
3. Tom's grandfather, Sir Geoffrey Shakespeare was made a baronet following his service as a Member of Parliament in the United Kingdom,
and in various senior government roles.
4. https://farmerofthoughts.co.uk/collected_pieces/plays-graves-and
-automobiles/
5. https://farmerofthoughts.co.uk/collected_pieces/pass-it-on/
6. https://farmerofthoughts.co.uk/speech-university-sunderland-honorary
-degree-ceremony/
7. https://farmerofthoughts.co.uk/collected_pieces/difficult-choices/

Patrick Flanagan

8. Acceptance to university in Ireland can be highly competitive, determined by the "points race," which refers to the number of points from
the student's performance in the final state examination at secondary
school, and the relative demand for their course/university choice.

Haraldur Thorleifsson

1. Figma. (2020, October 7). [YouTube]. https://www.youtube.com/watch
?v=WBB7A9kbH-k&feature=emb_logo
2. "Hustle culture" is an American term referring to young people who
are constantly working. It implies people are spending as much time
as possible working and earning a high degree of respect for their work
ethic.
3. Thorleifsson, H. (2019, January 15). Five years, that's not too long. Ueno.
https://loremipsum.ueno.co/five-years-thats-not-too-long-8af70f483bef

4. Thorleifsson, H. [@iamharaldur].(2020, December 27). *I have been in design and tech for over 20 years* [Tweet]. Twitter. https://twitter.com/iamharaldur/status/1343311852391030790?s=21

5. Thorleifsson, H. [@iamharaldur].(2021, February 20). *Who are some of your favorite people with disabilities in product design leadership?* [Tweet]. https://twitter.com/iamharaldur/status/1363171431622787075?s=20

6. Thorleifsson, H. (2021, January 6). 24,895 hours later. Ueno. https://loremipsum.ueno.co/24-895-hours-later-8286a1823dfd

Cathryn Gray

1. Star94. *Your positive athlete: Meet Cathryn Gray [Audio podcast episode]*. Radio.com. https://www.audacy.com/star94atlanta/blogs/jenn-friends/your-positive-athlete-meet-cathryn-gray

2. Homecoming and prom court are American traditions. Prior to the annual homecoming reunion and prom dance, students vote to identify three to four leaders in their school year, named to the court.

3. Trading pins is a tradition at major international sporting events; the lapel-style pins are generally representative of the countries the athletes come from.

4. University of Michigan. (2021). Providing adaptive sports. https://medicine.umich.edu/dept/family-medicine/programs/mdisability/providing-adaptive-sports

5. University of Michigan. (2021). Adaptive sports scholar: Cathyrn Gray. https://medicine.umich.edu/dept/family-medicine/adaptive-sports-scholar-cathryn-gray

6. Promising athletes frequently are awarded scholarships to attend college in the United States, but the large majority go to athletes without disabilities.

Robin Barnett

1. British Embassy Dublin. (2019, December 3). *A message from Ambassador Robin Barnett on International Day of Persons with Disabilities* [Facebook video]. https://www.facebook.com/BritishEmbassyDublin/videos/428114914807581

2. Independent.ie (2020, June 18). 'I wouldn't admit my disability until I realised the good it could do for others.' https://www.independent.ie/business/i-wouldnt-admit-my-disability-until-i-realised-the-good-it-could-do-for-others-39294346.html

3. Independent.ie (2020, September 20). 'I will never forget the murder of Lyra McKee. It was a reminder that some never accepted peace.' https://www.independent.ie/opinion/comment/i-will-never-forget-the-murder-of-lyra-mckee-it-was-a-reminder-that-some-never-accepted-peace-39545229.html

Tanni Grey-Thompson

1. DBE, Dame Commander of the Most Excellent Order of the British Empire, is a title bestowed on notable citizens of the British Empire.

2. Grey-Thompson, T. (2020). *Seize the Day: The story of a heroine of our time*. Hodder and Stoughton, 14.

3. *Seize the Day*, 22.

4. *Seize the Day*, 12.

5. Wheelchair slalom is an event that sees participants navigating through a course with challenging obstacles.

6. Adapted from *Seize the Day*.

7. *Seize the Day*, 47.

8. A crossbench peer is a non-political, independent position in the House of Lords, the UK's Upper House of Parliament. The word "crossbenchers" is derived from the benches that cross the chamber and sit perpendicular to other benches where government and opposition party members sit.

9. Grey-Thompson, T. (2012). *Aim High*. Headline Accent, 8.

Justin Gallegos

1. Elevation0m (2018, October 6). [YouTube]. Justin Gallegos. https://www.youtube.com/watch?v=x4KC0nUmY4Y

2. UO SOJC (2018, January 17). [YouTube]. Justin Gallegos: Stronger every minute. https://www.youtube.com/watch?v=Mp5SPZyeyps

3. Zoommagic (2018, October 6). Instagram. https://www.instagram.com/p/BonKcgiACIN/

4. Kipchoge, E. (2018, October 10). *Congratulations Justin, you earned it!* [Tweet]. Twitter. https://twitter.com/eliudkipchoge/status/1050367768854482944?lang=en

5. Kuzma, C. (2019, October 11). Keep striding forward: Pro runner with cerebral palsy makes marathon debut. *Runner's World*. https://www.runnersworld.com/runners-stories/a29404197/justin-gallegos-marathon-debut-chicago/

6. BBYO, formerly the B'nai B'rith Youth Organization, is a Jewish teen movement.

7. BBYO Insider (2019, February 25). [YouTube]. BBYO IC 2019 Plenary Speakers. https://www.youtube.com/watch?v=5pWF2--BdEU&feature=emb_logo

8. Zoommagic (2020). Instagram. https://www.instagram.com/p/CGONry1gyDG/

9. https://www.linkedin.com/in/justin-gallegos-031135133/

10. CPARF (2019, October 8). Nike's first professional athlete with cerebral palsy galvanized STEPtember campaign. https://cparf.org/sstposts/StoryId1570493710938

11. Collison, L. (2020). *Spastic Diplegia—Bilateral Cerebral Palsy*. Gillette Children's Press, 265.

Rachel Wobschall

1. Collison, L. (2020). *Spastic Diplegia—Bilateral Cerebral Palsy*. Gillette Children's Press, 266-8.

2. Novacheck, T.F., & Schwartz, M.H. (2020). *Improving Quality of Life for Individuals with Cerebral Palsy through Treatment of Gait Impairment: International Cerebral Palsy Function and Mobility Symposium*. Mac Keith Press.

Elizabeth Kolbe Hardcastle

1. Kolbe, C. (2019). *Struggling with Serendipity*. Eliezer Tristan Publishing, 145.

2. *Struggling with Serendipity*, 17-18.

3. *Struggling with Serendipity*, 15.

4. *Struggling with Serendipity*, 65.

Lightning Source UK Ltd.
Milton Keynes UK
UKHW011832300621
386412UK00001B/3

ABOUT THE AUTHORS

LILY COLLISON is the parent of three adult sons, the youngest of whom has spastic diplegia (a form of cerebral palsy). She previously worked in education and industry and is author of *Spastic Diplegia—Bilateral Cerebral Palsy*, published in 2020 by Gillette Children's Healthcare Press. She lives in Ireland with her husband.

KARA BUCKLEY is Senior Advi to the U.S. Olympic & Paralym Committee. She previously hel position of Global Director a leading partnerships with Oly and Paralympians. She lives ir with her husband and two c